THE MUST-HAVE PALEO DIET SLOW COOKER COOKBOOK

101 Super Easy And Delicious Paleo Diet Crock Pot Recipes For Rapid Weight Loss And A Better Life

Jamie Tolle

Contents

INTRODUCTION..1

PALEO DIET..3

THE DEFINITION...3
HEALTH BENEFITS OF PALEO DIET...3
HOW DOES PALEO HELP IN WEIGHT LOSS?................................4
WHAT CHANGES IN THE BODY WHILE ON PALEO DIET................5
DO'S & DON'TS OF PALEO DIET..5
FOODS TO AVOID OR TO INCLUDE..6

SLOW COOKER/CROCK-POT...8

BRIEF OVERVIEW OF SLOW COOKER..8
ADVANTAGES OF A SLOW COOKER...9
HOW DOES A SLOW COOKER WORK?..9
HOW TO CHOOSE A GOOD SLOW COOKER.................................10
QUICK TIPS..11

DELICIOUS RECIPES..13

1. Paleo Crock Pot Chicken Soup...13
2. Paleo Slow Cooker Fajita Soup...14
3. Slow Cooker Italian Meatball Soup.....................................15
4. Paleo Slow Cooker Carrot Butternut Soup.......................... 17
5. Paleo Slow Cooker French Onion Soup................................18
6. Paleo Thai Chicken Soup... 19
7. Slow Cooker Tom Kha Yum Soup....................................... 20
8. Paleo Crock Pot Bacon Soup... 21
9. Paleo Poblano Pumpkin Chili Soup..................................... 22
10. Paleo Slow Cooker Sweet Potato Chipotle Chili................. 23

STEWS.. 25

11. Paleo Crock Pot Beef Stew.. 25
12. Spicy Paleo Chinese Beef Stew...26
13. Paleo Crock Pot Irish Stew...27
14. Moroccan Lemon Beef Stew... 29

15. Paleo Chili Turkey Stew...30

CHILIES...31

16. Paleo Crock Pot Beef Chili...31
17. Paleo Slow Cooker Pork Chili..32
18. Paleo Meat & Veggies Chili..33

BEEF...35

19. Slow Cooker Thai Beef Stew..35
20. Crock Pot Beef Stroganoff...36
21. Paleo Spicy Beef Curry..37
22. Beef Bourguignon..38
23. Paleo Beef BBQ..39
24. Paleo Bacon Cabbage Chuck Beef Stew...40
25. Paleo Low Carb Beef Stew..41
26. Paleo Slow Cooker Shredded Beef...43
27. Paleo Middle Eastern Beef...44
28. Paleo Mexican Beef Stew...45
29. Paleo Drunken Beef Stew...46
30. Paleo Crockpot Spicy Indian Beef Roast...47

PORK...49

31. Paleo Crock Pot Spicy Pork Ribs...49
32. Easy BBQ Crock Pot Pork Ribs..50
33. Paleo Mushroom Pork Stew..51
34. Crock Pot Low Carb Pulled Pork..52
35. Crock Pot Chinese Spare Ribs..53
36. Paleo Easy Kalua Pork...54
37. Paleo Easy Baby Back Ribs...55
38. Slow Cooker Pork Tacos..56
39. Paleo Slow Cooker Meatloaf..57
40. Paleo Pork Shanks...58

LAMB...60

41. Paleo Lamb Stew...60
42. Paleo Lamb Roast Root Veggies...61

43. Slow Cooker Lamb Curry Stew...62

44. Paleo Crock Pot Leg of Lamb..63

45. Crock Pot Lamb Shanks...64

46. Graceful Paleo Lamb Stew...66

47. Paleo Lemon Artichoke Lamb...67

48. Parsley Butter Roasted Lamb...68

49. Slow Cooker Lamb Gizzard..69

50. Slow Cooker Lamb Cacciatore...70

CHICKEN

CHICKEN...71

51. Paleo Slow Cooker Chicken Curry..71

52. Crock Pot Stuffed Chicken Breasts..72

53. Crock Pot Chicken Hearts...73

54. Paleo Honey Chicken Drumsticks..74

55. Paleo Rosemary Lemon Chicken...75

56. Slow Cooker Rotisserie Chicken..76

57. Paleo Salsa Chicken...77

58. Paleo Crock Pot Turmeric Chicken..78

59. Paleo Crock Pot Marinara Chicken..79

60. Paleo Chocolate Chicken..80

61. Paleo Coconut Curried Chicken..81

62. Crock Pot Buffalo Chicken...82

63. Crock Pot Teriyaki Chicken..83

64. Crock Pot Pulled BBQ Chicken...84

65. Paleo Lemon Thyme Chicken...85

66. Paleo Slow Cooker Chicken Musakhan...86

SEAFOOD

SEAFOOD..88

67. Paleo Crock Pot Chicken & Shrimp...88

68. Paleo Salmon Head Soup...89

SIDE DISHES – STOCK - SAUSAGES

SIDE DISHES – STOCK - SAUSAGES..91

69. Paleo Crock Pot Applesauce...91

70. Crock Pot Sweet Potato Poi Poi Uala..92

71. Crockpot Split Pea Soup...92

72. Paleo Simple Slow Cooker Applesauce..94

73. Paleo Simple Vegetable Soup...94

74. Easy Crock Pot Mexican Stew.. 95

75. Paleo Crock Pot Summer Veggies.. 96

VEG / VEGAN...98

76. Slow Cooker Fig Apple Butter... 98

77. Paleo Easy Cabbage Apples...99

78. Crock Pot Vegetable Korma... 100

79. Paleo Cauliflower Pumpkin Lentils..101

80. Paleo Crock Pot Sarson Da Saag..102

81. Paleo Jambalaya Vegan... 103

82. Paleo Easy Mashed Potatoes.. 104

83. Paleo Easy Vegetable Casserole... 105

84. Paleo Vegetable Stew..106

85. Paleo Crock Pot Vegetable Curry..107

86. Paleo Easy Mexican Minestrone...108

WEEKEND / FESTIVE RECIPES.. 110

87. Paleo Easy Short Ribs... 110

88. Paleo Juicy Cuban Pork...111

89. Crock Pot Balsamic Pork...112

SPECIAL OCCASION RECIPES.. 113

90. Paleo Easy Vegetable Lasagna... 113

91. Paleo Crock Pot Sugar Ham..114

92. Slow Cooker Pumpkin Red Lentils Chili..115

DESSERTS...116

93. Crock Pot Maple Glazed Pecans...116

94. Paleo Cinnamon Apple Quinoa...117

95. Paleo Crockpot Pumpkin Butter...118

96. Paleo Poached Pears.. 119

97. Paleo Pumpkins Apples Raisins...120

98. Slow Cooker Brownie Bites...121

WICKED RECIPES.. 123

99. Paleo Chunky Monkey Crock Pot Trail Mix...123
100. Paleo Slow Cooker Carnitas.. 124
101. Paleo Jerk Styled Chicken...125

CONCLUSION...127

Introduction

Tired of being fat, sluggish, and in a bad mood?
Are you in Paleo Diet or interested in it? Do you have a Slow Cooker?
Do you want to combine both Paleo Diet and Slow Cooker to have flavored dishes and have a healthier lifestyle? **If yes, then this book is for you!**

Firstly, this book will tell you the essentials of Paleo diet, which is also known as cavemen's diet or primal diet. Paleo Diet is very popular nowadays. It is based on the food and diet habits that our ancestors used to follow, such as fruits, nuts, vegetables, and meat, meantime eliminate dairy, sugars, salt, alcohol and other processed foods.

So what benefits will you get from a Paleo Diet?
1. Long term and sustained weight loss
2. Feeling Satiety
3. Reducing body inflammation
4. Strengthens our immune system
5. Decrease the production of LDL
6. More and more...

By reading this book, you will not only get all above benefits from A Paleo Diet, you will also know how paleo diet help in weight loss, what will change in our body while on paleo diet, useful tips of paleo diet, foods to eat and avoid, etc..

Secondly, this book will tell you something important about Slow cooker, which is also referred to as Crock Pot, is a kitchen appliance, used for cooking through means of electricity. By using a slow cooker, you can just put the foods aside and can still work, sleep or go anywhere, and then after some hours you will have a very delicious and nutritional foods. **It will save you too much time, meantime serve you very mouth-watering recipes.**
In the book, you will know the essentials of slow cooker, how it works, how to choose a good one, how to maintenance it, and some very useful tips of using it, etc..

The biggest part of this book is the recipes. You will find **101** easy and great recipes, including stews, chili, lamb, pork, beef, chicken, vegetable, soup, seafood, desserts, weekend or festive recipes, special occasion recipes, and wicked recipes, etc.. You will find your favorite ones! All the recipes are in detailed step-by-step procedure, and the ingredients are easy to find in local market. All you need to do is just purchase the ingredients and put them into the slow cooker, then waiting some hours, you will finally have very tasty foods.

Hope this book will help you! Welcome to the Paleo Diet Slow Cooker World! Keep on reading...

Paleo Diet

The Definition

Paleo diet, which is known by several other names such as cavemen's diet or primal diet is immensely well received in today's age and time. It is based on the food and diet habits that our ancestors used to follow, such as fruits, nuts, vegetables, and meat. It is believed that by following Paleolithic diet, or popularly known as Paleo diet, we align our food habits with the digestive abilities of our ancestors.

It is completely based on the elimination of dairy, sugars, salt, and alcohol. Its increased popularity as a measure to improve overall health with better nutrition as it has a healthy ratio of fatty acids, improves the absorption of vitamin and various nutrients, and consists of an ideal balance of all the macro nutrients (Protein, Carb and Fat).

In no way does the Paleo diet mean an ordinary diet. It is more of a lifestyle that once you achieve your goal weight you are expected to stay on the diet plan. You would have to cut out processed foods to reap the benefits of the diet plan.

Health Benefits of Paleo Diet

1. As mentioned earlier, Paleo Diet helps in **striking the right balance between saturated and unsaturated fat**. Since the cells in our body is made up of both, it provides a perfect equilibrium, unlike other diet plans that stress on consumption of neither of them.
2. Rather than facilitating temporary **weight loss**, Paleo Diet is a long-term program that provides sustained results.
3. **Satiety** is one of the most outstanding benefits of Paleo diet. The choice of food in the plan is such that upon following this diet you tend to have

less food cravings, and in turn tend to eat less frequently. This also results on reducing emotional eating as you feel full longer.

4. As Paleo diet focuses on consumption of nuts and vegetables it leads to better intake of all the nutrients as well as striking a balance of Omega-3 and Omega-6 fatty acids which in turn assists in **reducing body inflammation**.

5. Paleo lifestyle also **improves tolerance of glucose in the body and improves sensitivity to insulin**.

6. Another notable benefit of the program is the inclusion of various fruits and vegetables in our diet and it **strengthens our immune system** which helps keep bad health at bay.

7. Paleo diet is also said to **decrease the production of LDL**, i.e., bad cholesterol in the body, and possibly reducing heart-related diseases.

8. As the program relies on meat to a greater extent, along with it comes protein, the building block of our body that helps in **building newer muscle cells**.

9. It offers a spectrum of vitamins and minerals through its diet plan, thus, takes improving the micronutrients the **body requires to function at the optimum**.

How Does Paleo Help In Weight Loss?

Most important factor that leads to weight loss while following Paleo diet is consumption of lesser calories, which in other words creates a caloric deficit in our body, without having to restrict them consciously.

Consumption of non-starchy vegetables, whole food carb choices and healthy fats leads to shedding body fat. Additionally, as the food choices are fulfilling, it further aids in eating less, without fighting appetite or counting each calorie. Tweaking intake of carbohydrates by lessening it leads to glycogen depletion and the body burns the fat reservoirs for survival.

What changes in the body while on Paleo Diet

- While religiously following the Paleo diet plan you tend to consume more protein and healthy fat, and avoid over consumption of carbohydrates. This helps build muscle and contribute to weight loss.
- Paleo diet leads to production of bacteria in the gut that aids in better digestion. Also, restriction of sugary foods and refined carbohydrates strengthens the digestive system.
- Foods in this diet are full of nutrients that promote regulation of hormones in the body and assists in detoxifying the body.
- It helps in reducing inflammation by consuming foods rich in fatty acids, like seeds, nuts, and raw vegetables.
- Having fish, beef, bone broth, broccoli, cauliflower in your diet provides enough calcium and magnesium to keep bones healthy.
- Paleo diet is rich in food that offers optimal intake of vitamin A and vitamin E, as well as zinc that contributes to better skin.
- Having good amounts of iron and protein in your diet promotes good hair health and stronger nails.
- As a result of feeling satisfied, you will eat less food.
- It is believed to reduce gluten tolerance/wheat tolerance.

Do's & Don'ts Of Paleo Diet

- Include plenty of protein in the diet, for instance beef, chicken, seafood, lamb, fish, pork.
- Include eggs in your meals. Do not restrict the consumption of egg yolks as cholesterol in them helps in better production of omega fatty acids that helps in hormone regulation.
- Eat plenty of vegetables while on Paleo diet. Green vegetables such as broccoli, cauliflower, spinach, bell peppers should be a part of most meals.
- Focus on eating good fat; some good sources are almonds, avocado, cashews and hazelnuts.
- In the case of grass fed animals, eating fat should not be a problem, however, opt for lean meats.

- Eat modest amounts of fruits throughout the day while focussing on berries.
- Completely avoid starchy vegetables, such as sweet potato, if you have a weight loss goal in mind.
- Avoid grains while following Paleo diet as it leads to over indulging, and inflammation in the body.
- Avoid all sugars while following the program. The only mode of sugar should be fructose, however, that should be limited in cases of a weight loss regime.
- Avoid legumes, as they also cause over consumption of food.
- Avoid seed oils of all forms and replace them with coconut oil or ghee.
- Avoid processed forms of dairy products, or restrict it to occasional consumption while on Paleo diet.

Foods To Avoid Or To Include

What foods should be on your plate?

The following is the list of food that should be consumed while following Paleo diet:
- Meat: Beef, pork, sheep, goat, rabbit, buffalo, turkey, seafood.
- Vegetables: Artichoke, cabbage, cucumber, parsley, parsnip, turnip, pumpkin, zucchini, cauliflower, eggplant, beets, carrots, mushroom, lettuce, kale, spinach, broccoli, celery, onions, asparagus, tomato.
- Fruits: Apple, banana, cantaloupes, figs, grapefruit, honeydew, lime, mango, papaya, pears, berries, plum, watermelon, apricot, cherries, guava, kiwi, lemon, orange, litchi, passion fruit, pomegranate, star fruit, tangerine, avocado, cherimoya, grapes, pears, pineapple.
- Seeds & Nuts: avocado oil, macadamia nut oil, cashew, macadamia nuts, pumpkin seeds, butter, olive oil, cashews, pecans, sunflower seeds, coconut, almonds, hazelnuts, pine nuts, walnuts.

Foods to avoid while on Paleo Diet:
- Dairy products: Butter, ice cream, cheese, milk, yogurt, pudding.
- Fruit Juice: apple juice, mango juice, cranberry juice, grape juice, orange juice.
- Soft drinks, soda, corn syrup, energy drinks and artificial sweetener.

- Grains & Legumes: Beans, cereals, crackers, corn syrup, miso, peanut butter, sandwiches, toasts, beer, kidney beans, oatmeal, pinto beans, sugar snap peas, bread, lentils, pancake, snow peas, wheat thins, chickpeas, soybeans, tofu, wheat, corn, peanuts, cream of wheat, mesquite, pasta, peas.

Tips:
- Although you wouldn't have to count calories as the food choices in the program would take care of frequent hunger, a calorie deficit is a prime requirement for successful weight loss through Paleo.
- Rather than focusing on what not to eat, focus on what to eat as it will open doors to an entire new world of eating habits and experiences.
- Try new plans among the food choices available, find out what works for you and create better plans until the desired outcome is achieved.
- Focus on body movements through the day, in the absence of any physical exercise or workout.
- Have a sound sleep routine.
- Keep a note of body progression while in different stages of the diet to ensure you are on the right track.

As with all recipes, it should be noted that when using your crock pot you should take into consideration that cooking times may vary. When trying a recipe for the first time, keep a closer eye on the cooking process, to ascertain time and heat level are accurate for thorough cooking.

SLOW COOKER/CROCK-POT

BRIEF OVERVIEW OF SLOW COOKER

Slow cooker, also referred to as Crock Pot, is a kitchen appliance, used for cooking through means of electricity. It uses the cooking technique of preparing the food in a hot liquid for an extended period. It prepares the food at a lower temperature, which cooks it thoroughly and healthier. Slow cookers don't demand your full attention. You can place all the ingredients into the pot, and let it do its thing. Slow cookers can be used to prepare a wide variety of dishes.

The idea of conceiving such a cooking utensil, the slow cooker, was developed by Irving Naxon, inspired by his grandmother. The idea was later bought by Radiant Heat Corp, New Jersey, which re-introduced it with a new name, Crock-Pot.

It gained quite a lot of popularity in early 70s, as women of the US stepped out of the home and began to work, and having a slow cooker eased the burden of meal preparation.

A slow cooker typically has a round shaped or oval shaped cooking pot, which is usually made of porcelain or ceramic with a metal body of the same shape surrounding it. The body contains the heating element to produce electricity.

The pot is covered with a glass lid while being prepared in a slow cooker. It comes in different sizes ranging in capacity of 2 cups to 30 cups. It is available with different heat settings.

ADVANTAGES OF A SLOW COOKER

There are many advantages of cooking with a crock pot a.k.a. slow cooker; however, you should know that this too, like other conventional ways of cooking, requires preparation. Meats should be browned on a stove, vegetables to be cleaned washed, chopped, minced and/or diced. Once you place the ingredients in the slow cooker, all you have to do is configure the time and temperature, and forget about it for a couple of hours. The best part is that post cooking the food, it changes the heat setting to warm.

Mostly fresh vegetables, meat, and other ingredients are used in a slow cooker for extended hours at low temperature. As a result, it brings out the natural flavor of the food, natural juice and nutrition are preserved, which leads to a healthy body and mind.

The use of a slow cooker isn't restricted to any particular time or season of the year. It can be used year round. In summertime, it saves from having to use the oven. It uses considerably less energy as compared to other conventional cooking devices. Post preparation of the meal, you wouldn't even have to clean a lot, as a slow cooker consists of just a pot. Variety of different foods can be cooked with a slow cooker, such as stews, casseroles, and soups.

HOW DOES A SLOW COOKER WORK?

In order to use a slow cooker, you are required to place raw ingredients; meat, vegetables, herbs, seasoning, sauces, along with a liquid, usually a third less than its alternatives, such as water, wine, or broth in the cooker. Place the lid on the cooker and desired settings.

Some of the cookers switch it's settings from 'cook' to 'warm' by itself, as a result of the cooking time is completed or the internal temperature of the food reached its cooked level.

The vapor produced as a result of the heat sticks to the lid of the cooker and returns into the cooker, which also maintains a higher level of the vitamin content. This liquid also continues the process of transferring the heat from the wall of the cooker to its ingredients which assists in even distribution of the flavor.

The lid also serves as containing the vapor.

Generally, with the basic ones, you are required to switch from one heat mode to another manually, however, in the advanced cookers, you can pre-set the heat requirement.

Low heat settings while cooking also results in delicate and tender dishes. The true luxury is to forget all about cooking for hours, until it is time to eat.

HOW TO CHOOSE A GOOD SLOW COOKER

If you have decided to procure a slow cooker because of the many benefits, or replacing your old one, here are a few things to consider before buying.

- They come in a variety of options; based on pricing and functionality. Choosing the right slow cooker for yourself should depend on your own needs, or how you plan to use it.
- Avoid choosing a slow cooker that has the crock set on top of the heating element, as it obstructs the heat being distributed equally and calls for frequent stirring. It is recommended to purchase a slow cooker with the heating element placed on either side of the base.
- They are offered in various materials, such as porcelain, metal, or ceramic. Although it really depends on individual preference, it is recommended to purchase one where the slow cooker and heating element are not attached, this will enhance the ease of cleaning your slow cooker, and entice people to use it more often when it is less cumbersome to clean.
- Choose a slow cooker with a glass lid. It offers an easier view into the slow cooker as the meal cooks.
- Shape of the cooker as well depends on personal preference. Though it is easier to cook meat in oval shaped cookers.
- They come in different sizes so while choosing the cooker you should keep in mind the quantity of dish to be prepared, based on the family size. A size of 6 quartz is usually preferred for household, as the cooker should not be more than half full while cooking to obtain the best cooking results.

- Buying a cooker with a timer, either a digital or with a pre-set time for cooking is also preferred, as it saves you from the hassle of being physically present while the dish is cooking. Additionally, slow cookers with a timer switches off by itself, once the cook time is completed and leaves a dish ready to serve.
- Some of the cookers also come with an inbuilt warming function, which keeps the dish warm once the set time is complete. This mode keeps the dish warm enough for consumption.

QUICK TIPS

- As we know the primary benefit of a slow cooker is how easy it is to use, it is recommended to complete any preparation beforehand, such as briefing cooking vegetables, like onions, leeks, or garlic to release their aromatic. Browning meat in a skillet beforehand adds a crust to the meat, which seals in juices as it cooks in the slow cooker. However, it is not necessary to sear meat prior to slow cooking. The low and slow process of cooking in a slow cooker adds to the flavor already.
- In cases where you might be short of time, complete the preparation the night before and place the ingredients in a zip lock bag, and refrigerator overnight. When you are close to adding the ingredients to the slow cooker, remove the baggie from the fridge to bring the ingredients to room temperature. It enhances the cooking process and flavor.
- Slow cookers are also money-savers. They afford you the option of cooking with a cheaper cut of meat, as the low and slow process of cooking enhances the tenderness and flavor in the meat.
- Adding oil or having fat to the meat isn't required in a slow cooker. It is advised to trim off the fat prior to cooking. This would also result in a healthier meal.
- Slow cooker requires less water than conventional cookers as the liquid which evaporates, stays inside, hence, having the cooker filled up half or two-thirds at the maximum is sufficient.
- It is also advised to use the low heat settings more often than other settings as it really brings out the best flavor of the ingredients and keeps the natural juices intact.

- Though it is recommended to choose recipes that require you to place all the ingredients at the same time, in some cases rice, certain herbs, pasta, might need to be added towards the latter half of the process.
- Root vegetables can take longer to cook than some meats, and it is advised to place them at the bottom of the cooker.

Delicious Recipes

1. Paleo Crock Pot Chicken Soup

Cook Time: 6 hrs

Servings: 4-6

INGREDIENTS

- 1 medium onion, diced
- 3 carrots, diced
- 3 celery stalks, diced
- 1 Tablespoon herbes de Provence
- 2 chicken thighs, organic, with bone, with skin
- 2 chicken breasts, organic, with bone, with skin
- 1 teaspoon apple cider vinegar
- 1 teaspoon sea salt
- ½ teaspoon fresh ground pepper
- 4 cups filtered water

DIRECTIONS:

1. Place all the ingredients in the crock pot, ensuring the chicken is placed on top of the vegetables, bone side down.
2. Add 4 cups of water, to cover the ingredients.
3. Cook on low for 6 hours, until meat flakes off bone and vegetables are fork tender.
4. Once cooked, take out the chicken. Remove skin and bones.
5. Shred the chicken with 2 forks.
6. Return pieces to the soup. Stir well.
7. Taste. Season if needed.
8. Serve in bowls.

Nutrition Facts (Per Serving)

393 Calories

7.8g Fat

2.3g Saturated Fat

0g Trans Fat
73mg Cholesterol
1041mg Sodium
719mg Potassium
53.2g Carbohydrates
7.8g Fiber
31.33g Sugars
25.5g Protein

2. Paleo Slow Cooker Fajita Soup

Cook Time: 4 hrs
Servings: 4-6

INGREDIENTS

- 1 ½ - 2 pounds chicken, boneless, skinless
- 1 yellow bell pepper, diced
- 1 red bell pepper, diced
- 1 green pepper, diced
- 1 medium onion, diced
- ½ jalapeño pepper, seeds removed, diced
- 2 garlic cloves, diced
- 1 cup salsa
- 4 cups chicken broth
- 1 Tablespoon chili powder
- 1 teaspoon paprika
- 1 teaspoon olive oil
- 1 teaspoon sea salt
- 1 teaspoon cumin
- 1 teaspoon ground pepper
- Juice from 1 lime
Garnish: sour cream, cilantro

DIRECTIONS:

1. Rinse the chicken, pat dry. Dice into cubes.
2. Place the ingredients in your crock pot starting with the salsa then vegetables, and jalapeno.
3. Add the chicken.
4. Add the seasoning.
5. Pour in the chicken broth.
6. Cover and cook on low for 5 hours. Test the chicken doneness. Cook longer if needed.
7. Serve in bowls. Garnish with sour cream and cilantro.

Nutrition Facts (Per Serving)

867 Calories
33g Total Fat
8.9g Saturated Fat
0g Trans Fat
370mg Cholesterol
1453mg Sodium
1390mg Potassium
10.5g Carbohydrates
2.7g Dietary Fiber
5.3g Sugars
125.3g Protein

3. Slow Cooker Italian Meatball Soup

Cook Time: 6 hrs

Serving: 4-6

INGREDIENTS

- 1 pound ground beef
- 1 medium can diced tomatoes, organic
- ¼ cup organic tomato sauce
- 4 cups low-sodium chicken broth

- 5 slices bacon, chopped, uncooked
- 1 medium zucchini, chopped
- 2 garlic cloves, minced
- 1 medium yellow squash, chopped
- ½ medium onion, chopped
- 1 medium carrot, chopped
- 1 Tablespoon golden flax meal
- 1 Tablespoon coconut flour
- ½ teaspoon garlic powder
- ½ Tablespoon Italian seasoning
- 1 teaspoon garlic powder
- ½ teaspoon sea salt and fresh ground pepper, each

DIRECTIONS

1. In a large bowl, combine the ground beef, flax meal, coconut flour, garlic powder, and tomato paste.
2. Mix with the ingredients with your hands until combined.
3. Form meatballs, bit bigger than golf balls.
4. In a large skillet, brown the meatballs until they form a crust.
5. Place the rest of the ingredients in the slow cooker. Add the meatballs. Stir until combined.
6. Cover and cook on low for 6 hours. Test the doneness. Cook longer if necessary.
7. Serve in bowls. Garnish with grated parmesan cheese.

Nutrition Facts (Per Serving)

239 Calories
9.1g Total Fat
3.2g Saturated Fat
0g Trans Fat
74mg Cholesterol
1041mg Sodium
664mg Potassium
7.8g Carbohydrates
2.4g Dietary Fiber
3.3g Sugars
29.8g Protein

4. Paleo Slow Cooker Carrot Butternut Soup

Cook Time: 8 hrs

Serving: 2-4

INGREDIENTS

- 1 large butternut squash, peeled, cubed
- ½ medium onion, chopped
- 6-8 large carrots, chopped
- 3 cups vegetable broth
- 1 cup almond milk
- 3 slices bacon, cooked, crumbled
- 1 Tablespoon sesame seeds
- 4 Tablespoons pumpkin seeds
- 1 pinch ground cinnamon
- Oil to drizzle over vegetables before roasting
- 1 pinch sea salt, fresh ground pepper, each

DIRECTIONS

1. Preheat oven to 350°F.
2. Place all the chopped vegetables in a single layer on a baking sheet. Drizzle with oil. Season with salt and pepper.
3. Bake in the oven for 30 minutes. Turn after 15 minutes.
4. Add the roasted vegetables to your slow cooker.
5. Cover and cook on low for 5 hours, or until tender.
6. Once cooking completed. Add the almond milk, ground cinnamon.
7. Blend until smooth. Turn the heat to high, stirring for 5 minutes until soup is heated through.
8. Serve in bowls. Garnish with crumbled bacon, sesame seeds, and pumpkin seeds.

Nutrition Facts (Per Serving)
395 Calories
26.7g Total Fat
15.6g Saturated Fat
0g Trans Fat
10mg Cholesterol

692mg Sodium
1080mg Potassium
31.5g Carbohydrates
7.2g Dietary Fiber
10.5g Sugars
13.3g Protein

5. Paleo Slow Cooker French Onion Soup

Cook Time: 6 hrs

Serving: 2-4

INGREDIENTS

- 2 pounds sweet onions, sliced
- 3 cups chicken broth
- 3 cups beef broth
- 3 cups of water
- 1 1/2 teaspoons dried thyme
- 3 Tablespoons coconut oil
- ¼ teaspoon sea salt and fresh ground pepper, each
- 2-4 slices of bread
- 2-4 slices swiss cheese or gruyere

DIRECTIONS

1. Slice the sweet onions into thin pieces.
2. Place them in the slow cooker, drizzle coconut oil over the slices. Stir until coated.
3. Cook on low for 4 hours, to caramelize the sweet onions.
4. Add the broth, dried thyme, and water.
5. Cook on low for 2 hours.
6. Pour the onions and broth in oven-safe bowls.
7. Top with slice of bread. Top with cheese.
8. Place the bowls on a baking tray and slide under broiler until cheese is melted and golden brown.

Nutrition Facts (Per Serving)
343 Calories
12.9g Total Fat
9.1g Saturated Fat
0g Trans Fat
5mg Cholesterol
1347mg Sodium
158mg Potassium
42.7g Carbohydrates
14.6g Dietary Fiber
7g Sugars
16.5g Protein

6. Paleo Thai Chicken Soup

Cook Time: 6 hrs

Serving: 8-10

INGREDIENTS

- 4 pounds chicken
- 5 slices of fresh ginger, minced
- 20 fresh basil leaves, for crock pot and garnish
- 1 stalk lemongrass, chopped
- Juice of 1 lemon
- Pinch of sea salt and fresh ground pepper, each

DIRECTIONS

1. Place all the ingredients in your crock pot. Add water.
2. Cover and cook on low for 6 hours. Check doneness of chicken. Cook longer if necessary. Check at 30 minute intervals.
3. Serve in bowls. Garnish with basil.

Nutrition Facts (Per Serving)
450 Calories

mushrooms. Re-cover cook until they are fork tender.
4. Add cilantro leaves, serve the soup in bowls.

Nutrition Facts (Per Serving)
515 Calories
39.5g Total Fat
30.2g Saturated Fat
0g Trans Fat
67mg Cholesterol
1070mg Sodium
925mg Potassium
16g Carbohydrates
4.6g Dietary Fiber
7.9g Sugars
28.6g Protein

8. Paleo Crock Pot Bacon Soup

Cook Time: 5 hrs

Serving: 4-6

INGREDIENTS

- 6 cups beef broth
- 2 cups brussel sprouts, choppcd
- 3 cups sweet potatoes, chopped
- 2 cups mushrooms, chopped
- 1 Tablespoon olive oil
- 5 pieccs of bacon, cut into chunks
- 1 Tablespoon honey mustard
- 1 garlic clove, minced
- ½ teaspoon smoked paprika
- 1 Tablespoon dried herbs
- Pinch of sea salt, fresh ground pepper, each
Garnish: ¼ cup cheddar cheese, grated

DIRECTIONS

1. Chop the potatoes and brussel sprouts into equal chunks.
2. Add the brussel sprouts, bacon and beef broth to the slow cooker. Stir in tablespoon of oil.
3. Season the mixture. Stir well. Cover and cook on low for 3 hours.
4. After 4 hours, add the mushrooms and herbs. Stir well.
5. Cover and cook another 2 hours.
6. Serve in bowls. Garnish with grated cheese.

Nutrition Facts (Per Serving)

745 Calories
48.3g Total Fat
15.3g Saturated Fat
0g Trans Fat
116mg Cholesterol
3265mg Sodium
1479mg Potassium
27.8 g Carbohydrates
4.8g Dietary Fiber
8.7g Sugars
47.9g Protein

9. Paleo Poblano Pumpkin Chili Soup

Cook Time: 4 hrs

Serving: 4-6

INGREDIENTS

- 1 1/2 pounds ground beef, lean
- 1 cup beef broth
- 1 Poblano pepper
- 15 ounce can pumpkin puree (not pie mix)
- 1 cup diced sweet onion
- 2 garlic cloves, minced

- 15 ounce can diced tomatoes
- 1 Tablespoon tomato paste
- 2 Tablespoons cumin
- 2 Tablespoons chili powder
- 1 teaspoon cinnamon
- 1 teaspoon nutmeg
- 1 teaspoon sea salt, fresh ground pepper, each

Garnish: chopped parsley

DIRECTIONS

1. Preheat oven to 350∘F.
2. Place the Poblano pepper on a baking sheet, drizzle with oil. Bake for 10 minutes, until soft.
3. Peel the skin off the pepper. Chop it up.
4. Place ground beef, pepper, sweet onion, garlic, pumpkin puree, tomato paste, diced tomatoes in your slow cooker. Stir well.
5. Add beef broth. Add seasoning. Stir well.
6. Cover and cook on low for 4 hours, until meat and onion cooked through.
7. Serve in bowls. Garnish with parsley.

Nutrition Facts (Per Serving)
279 Calories
8.6g Total Fat
3g Saturated Fat
0g Trans Fat
101mg Cholesterol
551mg Sodium
918mg Potassium
14.1g Carbohydrates
4.9g Dietary Fiber
5.9g Sugars
37g Protein

10. Paleo Slow Cooker Sweet Potato Chipotle Chili

Cook Time: 4 hrs

Serving: 4-6

INGREDIENTS

- 1 pound ground pork, beef, or chicken
- 2 cups chicken or beef broth
- 3 sweet potatoes, chopped
- 3 cups cauliflower, chopped
- 1 white onion, chopped
- ½ red onion, chopped
- 2 chipotle peppers, minced
- 2 garlic cloves, minced
- 14 ounce can diced tomatoes
- ¼ teaspoon cumin
- ¼ teaspoon sea salt, fresh ground pepper, each
- ½ teaspoon paprika

Garnish: shallots or parsley

DIRECTIONS

1. Place the meat of choice, potatoes, cauliflower, white onions only, garlic, peppers, and diced tomatoes in your slow cooker.
2. Pour in the broth. Stir well.
3. Cover and cook on high for 4 hours, stirring occasionally.
4. Add red onions last hour of cooking.
5. Serve in bowls. Garnish with shallots or parsley.

Nutrition Facts (Per Serving)

334 Calories
17.1g Total Fat
1.3g Saturated Fat
0g Trans Fat
22mg Cholesterol
542mg Sodium
829mg Potassium
22.7g Carbohydrates
5g Dietary Fiber
4.9g Sugars
23.5g Protein

3. Add the broth, tomato paste. Stir well.
4. Cover and cook on low for approximately 8 hours.
5. If the mixture seems dry, add more broth.
6. Take out the bay leaf.
7. Serve in bowls.

Nutrition Facts (Per Serving)
232 Calories
4.8g Total Fat
0.8g Saturated Fat
0g Trans Fat
0mg Cholesterol
1044mg Sodium
567mg Potassium
41.6g Carbohydrates
6.1g Dietary Fiber
7.6g Sugars
6.8g Protein

12. Spicy Paleo Chinese Beef Stew

Cook Time: 6 hrs

Serving: 8-10

INGREDIENTS

- 1 pound stewing beef, chunks
- 4 cups beef broth
- 4 large carrots, chopped
- 4 celery stalks, chopped
- 1 large russet potato, chopped
- ¼ cup mushrooms, sliced
- 1 large onion, diced
- 1 Tablespoon avocado oil
  1 teaspoon Chinese 5-spice

- 2 teaspoon coconut sugar
- ½ teaspoon crushed pepper flakes
- ½ cup dry sherry
- 1 Tablespoon arrowroot powder

DIRECTIONS

Option: Brown the meat in a skillet then place in crock pot or place meat directly in crock pot (there isn't a very big difference in the cooking but the seared meat will have a slightly extra crunch from the crust.)

1. Drizzle the oil along the bottom of the crock pot.
2. Add the meat, carrots, celery, potato, mushrooms, onion, crushed pepper flakes, Chinese 5-spice, and coconut sugar to the crock pot. Stir well.
3. Pour in the broth and sherry. Add the seasoning. Stir well.
4. Cover and cook on low for 6 hours.
5. Stir in the arrowroot powder 1 hour prior to end of cooking.
6. Serve in bowls.

Nutrition Facts (Per Serving)
165 Calories
6.1g Total Fat
3.5g Saturated Fat
0g Trans Fat
41mg Cholesterol
540mg Sodium
497mg Potassium
10.6g Carbohydrates
1.7g Dietary Fiber
4.7g Sugars
16.5g Protein

13. Paleo Crock Pot Irish Stew

Cook Time: 6 hrs

Serving: 8-10

INGREDIENTS

- 2 pounds stewing beef, chunks
- 3 cups dark beer + 3 cups beer for marinating
- ½ cup arrowroot powder
- 5 carrots, chopped
- 5 yellow potatoes, chopped
- ½ head cabbage, sliced
- 28 ounce can diced tomatoes
- 2 medium onions, diced
- 4 garlic cloves, minced
- Pinch of sea salt and fresh ground pepper, each
- 3-4 cups chicken bone broth

Garnish: chopped parsley

DIRECTIONS

1. Chop up the stewing beef. Place in a large Ziploc baggie. Pour the beer in the baggie. Refrigerate the beef 12-24 hours.
2. After marinating, dump the beer. Place beef in crock pot.
3. Add the carrots, potatoes, cabbage, onions, garlic, salt, pepper.
4. Stir in the arrowroot flower until ingredients are coated.
5. Pour in the other 3 cups of beer. Stir until incorporated.
6. Cover and cook on low for approximately 6 hours. Test the doneness. Continue cooking. Check at 30 minute intervals.
7. Serve in bowls. Garnish with parsley.

Nutrition Facts (Per Serving)

1249 Calories
21.2g Total Fat
4.2g Saturated Fat
0g Trans Fat
84mg Cholesterol
1078mg Sodium
10557mg Potassium
231.6g Carbohydrates
52.8g Dietary Fiber
5.4g Sugars
71.2g Protein

14. Moroccan Lemon Beef Stew

Cook Time: 4 hrs

Serving: 4-6

INGREDIENTS

- 2 pounds stewing beef
- 1 medium butternut squash, diced
- 3 medium yellow onions, diced
- 3 garlic cloves, minced
- 2 Tablespoons ras el hanout spice
- 2 cups beef broth
- Juice from 2 lemons
- ⅓ cup butter
- Pinch of salt and fresh ground pepper, each

DIRECTIONS

1. Place all the ingredients but the squash in the slow cooker.
2. Cover and cook on medium for4 hours, until meat is tender.
3. Add the squash to the cooker. Cook for another hour.
4. Serve in bowls, over rice.

Nutrition Facts (Per Serving)

449 Calories
21.8g Total Fat
11g Saturated Fat
0g Trans Fat
174mg Cholesterol
1535mg Sodium
906mg Potassium
11g Carbohydrates
2.5g Dietary Fiber
3.4g Sugars
51.3g Protein

15. Paleo Chili Turkey Stew

Cook Time: 6 hrs
Serving: 8-10

INGREDIENTS

- 2 pounds ground turkey
- 3 garlic cloves, minced
- 1 large onion, diced
- Red and green peppers, diced
- 1 stalk of celery, diced
- 2 carrots, diced
- 1 jalapeno pepper, seeded and diced
- 14 ounce can diced tomatoes
- 28 ounce can crushed tomatoes
- 15 ounce can tomato sauce

DIRECTIONS

1. Sauté garlic and onion in a skillet.
2. Add onion, garlic with rest of ingredients to the crock pot.
3. Cook on low for 6 hours.
4. Serve hot. Garnish with avocado.

Nutrition Facts (Per Serving)

236 Calories
4.9g Total Fat
1.5g Saturated Fat
0g Trans Fat
69mg Cholesterol
797mg Sodium
744mg Potassium
16g Carbohydrates
4.3g Dietary Fiber
10.8g Sugars
31.3g Protein

CHILIES

16. Paleo Crock Pot Beef Chili

Cook Time: 6 hrs

Serving: 4-6

INGREDIENTS

- 2 pounds lean ground beef
- 4 garlic cloves, minced
- 1 medium onion, diced
- 1 green pepper, diced
- 1 red pepper, diced
- 1 tomato, diced
- 3 celery stalks, diced
- ¼ cup green chilies, diced
- 28 ounce can crushed tomatoes
- 2 Tablespoons chili powder
- 15 ounce can tomato sauce
- ½ Tablespoon basil
- 1 Tablespoon oregano
- ½ Tablespoon adobo sauce
- ½ Tablespoon cumin
- ½ teaspoon cayenne
- Pinch of sea salt, fresh ground pepper, each

DIRECTIONS

1. Add all the ingredients to your slow cooker. Stir until combined.
2. Cover and cook on low for 6 hours.
3. Serve in bowls. Garnish with cilantro. Side with tortilla chips

Nutrition Facts (Per Serving)

372 Calories

10.9g Total Fat
3.7g Saturated Fat
0g Trans Fat
135mg Cholesterol
948mg Sodium
1400mg Potassium
19.9g Carbohydrates
5.5g Dietary Fiber
7.4g Sugars
49.5g Protein

17. Paleo Slow Cooker Pork Chili

Cook Time: 6 hrs

Serving: 8-10

INGREDIENTS

- 4 pounds stewing beef
- 2 pounds pork shoulder
- 2 onions, chopped
- 2 cans diced tomatoes
- 1 teaspoon black pepper
- 6 garlic cloves, chopped
- 1 cup fresh chilies, finely chopped
- 3 Tablespoons smoked paprika
- 2 chipotle peppers, chopped
- 3 Tablespoons dark cocoa powder
- 2 Tablespoons ground cumin
- Pinch of sea salt, fresh ground pepper, each
Garnish: cilantro

DIRECTIONS

1. Chop up the beef and pork into chunks.
2. Add the onions, garlic, tomatoes, and chilies. Stir until combined.

3. Cover and cook on low for 6 hours. Check meat doneness. Continue cooking if needed. Check at 30 minute intervals.
4. Serve in bowls. Garnish with cilantro.

Nutrition Facts (Per Serving)
787 Calories
41g Total Fat
14.4g Saturated Fat
0g Trans Fat
228mg Cholesterol
388mg Sodium
1671mg Potassium
36.1g Carbohydrates
13.9g Dietary Fiber
19.3g Sugars
71.1g Protein

18. Paleo Meat & Veggies Chili

Cook Time: 6 hrs

Serving: 6-8

INGREDIENTS

- 1½ pounds lean ground beef
- 2 Tablespoons olive oil
- 2 garlic cloves, chopped
- 1 celery stalk, chopped
- 1 large onion, diced
- 1 carrot, diced
- 2 Tablespoons chili powder
- 1 teaspoon oregano
- 1 teaspoon ground cumin
- ¼ teaspoon cayenne pepper (optional)

- 15 ounce can tomato sauce
- 2 large zucchini, diced
- 15 ounce can diced tomatoes

Garnish: chopped parsley

DIRECTIONS

1. Place all the ingredients in your slow cooker.
2. Cover and cook on low for 6 hours, until meat is cooked and vegetables are fork tender.
3. Serve hot. Side with rice or bread.

Nutrition Facts (Per Serving)

721 Calories
23.7g Total Fat
7.9g Saturated Fat
0g Trans Fat
279mg Cholesterol
599mg Sodium
2185mg Potassium
25.3g Carbohydrates
6.7g Dietary Fiber
12.3g Sugars
98.5g Protein

BEEF

19. Slow Cooker Thai Beef Stew

Cook Time: 5 hrs

Serving: 6-8

INGREDIENTS

- 3 pounds stewing beef
- 2 Tablespoons coconut oil (for searing beef)
- 2 garlic cloves, minced
- 1 medium yellow onion, sliced
- 13.5 ounce can coconut milk, full fat
- 1 inch piece ginger, peeled and minced
- ⅓ cup tomato paste
- 2 Tablespoon fish sauce
- ½ cup Thai red curry paste
- 1 teaspoon sea salt
- 2 teaspoons fresh lime juice
- 2 cups carrots, diced
- 2 cups broccoli, diced
- 1 cup peeled jicama

DIRECTIONS

Option: Chop the stewing beef into bite-size chunks. Sear the stewing beef in a skillet with oil before placing in crock pot.

1. Cooked or uncooked, place the chunks of beef in the crock pot.
2. Add the other ingredients (not the oil, only use that for searing) to the crock pot. Stir until combined.
3. Cover and cook on low for 5 hours, until meat is done.
4. Serve warm. Side with rice and pita bread/naan.

Nutrition Facts (Per Serving)
540 Calories
27.5g Total Fat
16.6g Saturated Fat
0g Trans Fat
152mg Cholesterol
1757mg Sodium
1035mg Potassium
15.1g Carbohydrates
2.9g Dietary Fiber
5.1g Sugars
54.3g Protein

20. Crock Pot Beef Stroganoff

Cook Time: 5 hrs

Serving: 6-8

INGREDIENTS

- 2 pounds stewing beef
- 2 teaspoons paprika
- 2 teaspoons red wine vinegar
- 1 teaspoon garlic powder
- 1 teaspoon onion powder
- 1 teaspoon thyme
- ½ medium white onion, sliced
- ½ cup mushrooms, sliced
- ⅓ cup coconut cream
- Pinch of sea salt, fresh ground pepper, each

DIRECTIONS

tion: Chop the stewing beef into chunks. Sear the beef in a skillet before
  sferring to crock pot.

1. Place the mushrooms and onions in the bottom of the crock pot.
2. Place the meat, cooked or uncooked, on top of the vegetables.
3. Pour the seasoning over the meat. Pour the red wine vinegar in the crock pot.
4. Cover and cook on low for 5 hours.
5. Once the meat is cooked, turn the crock pot to high, add the cream. Stir until it thickens the sauce.
6. Serve warm. Side with noodles, rice, or naan bread.

Nutrition Facts (Per Serving)
330 Calories
12.8g Total Fat
6.4g Saturated Fat
0g Trans Fat
135mg Cholesterol
880mg Sodium
808mg Potassium
4.1g Carbohydrates
1.3g Dietary Fiber
1.8g Sugars
47.7g Protein

21. Paleo Spicy Beef Curry

Cook Time: 4 hrs

Serving: 8-10

INGREDIENTS

- 2.5 pounds beef chuck
- 2 Tablespoons curry powder
- 1 medium white onion, diced
- ½ inch piece of ginger, peeled and minced
- 3 garlic cloves, minced

- 2 cups whole fat coconut milk
- 2 Tablespoons chili sauce
- ½ teaspoon sea salt

DIRECTIONS

1. Place all the ingredients in the crock pot.
2. Cook on low for 4 hours.
3. Serve warm. Side with rice, pita bread/naan.

Nutrition Facts (Per Serving)

237 Calories
8.2g Total Fat
3.5g Saturated Fat
0g Trans Fat
101mg Cholesterol
385mg Sodium
508m Potassium
4.1g Carbohydrates
0.9g Dietary Fiber
2.2g Sugars
34.8g Protein

22. Beef Bourguignon

Cook Time: 5 hrs

Serving: 2-4

INGREDIENTS

- 1 pound chuck steak, sliced
- ¼ cup tapioca flour
- 2 cups dry red wine
- 1 teaspoon cumin powder
- 2 carrots, sliced

- ½ pound bacon
- 1 garlic clove, diced
- 2 large red onions, sliced
- 1 Savoy cabbage, sliced
- 1 cup beef bone broth
- 1 sprig thyme
- Pinch of sea salt and fresh ground pepper, each

DIRECTIONS

1. Cut the chuck roast into bite-size pieces.
2. Line the bottom of the crock pot with the bacon.
3. Add the meat with the other ingredients on top of the bacon, add the broth last.
4. Cook on low for 4-5 hours.
5. Serve in bowls. Side with a salad.

Nutrition Facts (Per Serving)
424 Calories
30.2g Total Fat
13.5g Saturated Fat
0g Trans Fat
104mg Cholesterol
596mg Sodium
121mg Potassium
7.6g Carbohydrates
1.9g Dietary Fiber
3.2g Sugars
31.6g Protein

25. Paleo Low Carb Beef Stew

Cook Time: 5-6hrs

Serving: 2-4

INGREDIENTS
- 1 pound stewing beef

- 2 medium turnips, chopped
- 1 medium onion, chopped
- 2 garlic cloves, minced
- 1/2 can tomato paste
- 2 medium carrots, chopped
- 4 sprigs of thyme
- 2 bay leaves
- 3 celery stalks, diced
- 2 Tablespoons apple cider vinegar
- 2 Tablespoons chopped parsley
- 3 cups green beans
- 1 Tablespoon arrowroot (or corn starch)
- Pinch of sea salt, fresh ground pepper, each

DIRECTIONS

1. Chop the stewing beef into chunks.
2. Place all ingredients (except the arrowroot) in your slow cooker.
3. Cook on low for 5 hours, until meat is cooked.
4. During the last hour of cooking, if the liquid is on the thin side, stir in some arrowroot flour.
5. Serve warm. Side with noodles or naan bread.

Nutrition Facts (Per Serving)

264 Calories
6.7g Total Fat
2.2g Saturated Fat
0g Trans Fat
41mg Cholesterol
140mg Sodium
1158mg Potassium
23.1g Carbohydrates
7.9g Dietary Fiber
9.8g Sugars
29.3g Protein

26. Paleo Slow Cooker Shredded Beef

Cook Time: 5 hrs

Serving: 6-8

INGREDIENTS

- 3.5 pounds chuck roast
- ¼ cup beef stock
- ½ Tablespoon oregano
- ¼ teaspoon ancho chile
- ½ teaspoon cumin
- ⅛ teaspoon cinnamon
- ¼ teaspoon paprika
- ½ teaspoon garlic
- 2 Tablespoon tomato paste
- Pinch of sea salt, fresh ground pepper, each

DIRECTIONS

1. In a large crock pot, add the meat, broth, and tomato paste.
2. Stir the ingredients so the meat is coated.
3. Sprinkle the seasoning over the meat.
4. Cover and cook on medium for 5 hours.
5. Once the meat has finished cooking, use two forks to shred.
6. Serve warm, on a bun or side with salad.

Nutrition Facts (Per Serving)

569 Calories

41.7g Total Fat

16.5g Saturated Fat

0g Trans Fat

167mg Cholesterol

347mg Sodium

489mg Potassium

3g Carbohydrates

1g Dietary Fiber

1.5g Sugars

43.2g Protein

27. Paleo Middle Eastern Beef

Cook Time: 6 hrs

Serving: 6

INGREDIENTS

- 3 pounds beef brisket, grass fed
- 1 teaspoon cloves
- 1 teaspoon fennel seeds
- 1 teaspoon cumin powder
- ½ teaspoon cloves
- ½ teaspoon cinnamon
- 1 teaspoon cardamom powder
- 3 Tablespoons tomato paste
- ¼ teaspoon sea salt
- 3 cups bone broth
- ½ large sweet onion, diced
- ¼ cup coconut vinegar
- Pinch of salt and fresh ground pepper

DIRECTIONS

1. Season the meat with salt and pepper
2. Sprinkle mixture of fennel seeds, cumin powder, cloves. Add the wet ingredients.
3. Cover and cook on medium for 6 hours. Shred with two forks once tender.
4. Serve warm. Side with rice.

Nutrition Facts (Per Serving)

263 Calories

9.2g Total Fat

3g Saturated Fat

0g Trans Fat

60mg Cholesterol

175mg Sodium

707mg Potassium

2.7g Carbohydrates

0.7g Dietary Fiber

2. After 4 hours of cooking, sauté the mushrooms and add to the crock pot. Cook for another hour.
3. 30 minutes before end of cooking add the arrowroot to the ingredients and stir.
4. Add the wine. Cook until the sauce is thickened.
5. Serve warm.

Nutrition Facts (Per Serving)

356 Calories
15g Total Fat
7g Saturated Fat
0g Trans Fat
96mg Cholesterol
378mg Sodium
673mg Potassium
13.3g Carbohydrates
3.4g Dietary Fiber
5.6g Sugars
33g Protein

30. Paleo Crockpot Spicy Indian Beef Roast

Cook Time: 6 hrs

Serving: 6-8

INGREDIENTS

- 2 ½ pounds beef roast
- 2 Tablespoons coconut oil
- 2 red onions, chopped
- 1 teaspoon black mustard seeds
- 20-30 curry leaves
- 2 garlic cloves, minced
- 2 Tablespoons fresh squeezed lemon juice
- 1 minced serrano pepper
- 1 ½ inch grated ginger

- 1 Tablespoon coriander powder
- 1 Tablespoon meat masala
- 1 teaspoon turmeric
- 2 teaspoons Kashmiri chili powder
- ¼ cup coconut slices
- 1 teaspoon salt
- ½ teaspoon fresh ground pepper

DIRECTIONS

1. Chop the beef into bite-size pieces.
2. Add mustard seeds, onions, oil, and salt in the crock pot.
3. Cover and cook on high for 1 hour.
4. Add remaining ingredients, except coconut slices, to the crock pot. Re-cover and cook on high for 4 hours.
5. After cooking, add slices of coconut.
6. Re-cover, cook on high for another hour.
7. Serve warm. Side with bread, rice.

Nutrition Facts (Per Serving)

204 Calories
7.8g Total Fat
5.8g Saturated Fat
0g Trans Fat
75mg Cholesterol
1029mg Sodium
78mg Potassium
4.1g Carbohydrates
1.1g Dietary Fiber
1.4g Sugars
30.8g Protein

PORK

31. Paleo Crock Pot Spicy Pork Ribs

Cook Time: 5-6 hrs
Serving: 10-12

INGREDIENTS

- 4 pounds pork ribs
- 2 teaspoons Chinese five-spice powder
- 1 jalapeño, cut in rings
- ¾ teaspoon granulated garlic powder
- 2 Tablespoons coconut Aminos
- 2 Tablespoons rice vinegar
- 1 Tablespoon tomato paste
- Pinch of salt and fresh ground pepper

DIRECTIONS

1. Chop the ribs up into smaller pieces, 3-4 strips.
2. Season with salt, pepper and 5-spice powder. Place in crock pot.
3. Add jalapeno, tomato paste, aminos and rice vinegar to the ingredients. Stir well.
4. Cover and cook on low for 5-6 hours, until ribs are tender.
5. Serve hot. Side with rice or noodles.

Nutrition Facts (Per Serving)

418 Calories
26.8g Total Fat
9.5g Saturated Fat
0.2g Trans Fat
156mg Cholesterol
89mg Sodium
465mg Potassium
0.7g Carbohydrates
0.3g Dietary Fiber

0.4g Sugars
40.2g Protein

32. Easy BBQ Crock Pot Pork Ribs

Cook Time: 6 hrs
Serving: 10-15

INGREDIENTS
- 6 pounds pork ribs
- ½ Tablespoon chipotle seasoning
- ½ Tablespoon chili powder
- ½ Tablespoon ancho chili pepper powder
- ¼ teaspoon cumin
- ¼ teaspoon cinnamon
- 1 large white onion, sliced
- Pinch of salt and fresh ground pepper, each
- 1 Tablespoon ghee
- 6 garlic cloves, crushed
- 2 cups Brian's Barbecue Sauce

DIRECTIONS
1. Cut the ribs into smaller pieces.
2. Season with ancho, chipotle, salt, cumin and pepper. Place in crock pot.
3. Add remaining ingredients in the crock pot. Stir.
4. Cover and cook on medium for 6 hours, until meat is tender.
5. Serve hot. Side with rice or salad.

Nutrition Facts (Per Serving)
480 Calories
28.8g Total Fat
10.4g Saturated Fat
0.2g Trans Fat
165mg Cholesterol
378mg Sodium
514mg Potassium
9.8g Carbohydrates

0.2g Dietary Fiber
6.7g Sugars
42.2g Protein

33. Paleo Mushroom Pork Stew

Cook Time: 6 hrs
Serving: 6-8

INGREDIENTS
- 2 pounds pork loin
- 2 pounds oyster mushrooms, chopped
- 2 Tablespoons coconut oil
- 1 garlic clove, chopped
- 1 medium onion, chopped
- ½ teaspoon salt and fresh ground pepper, each
- 2 Tablespoons dried mustard
- 2 Tablespoons dried oregano
- 1 ½ cups bone broth
- ½ teaspoon freshly nutmeg, grated
- 2 Tablespoons white wine vinegar
- ¼ cup ghee
- ¼ cup full fat coconut milk
- 3 Tablespoons capers

DIRECTIONS
1. Chop the pork loin into chunks.
2. Place the meat in crock pot. Add seasoning.
3. Add remaining ingredients but not mushrooms. Stir in the broth.
4. Cover and cook on low for 6 hours.
5. Add mushrooms in the last hour of cooking.
6. Serve warm. Side with mashed potatoes.

Nutrition Facts (Per Serving)
453 Calories
14.4g Total Fat

7.1g Saturated Fat
0g Trans Fat
57mg Cholesterol
184mg Sodium
381mg Potassium
36.5g Carbohydrates
7.2g Dietary Fiber
0.5g Sugars
41.1g Protein

34. Crock Pot Low Carb Pulled Pork

Cook Time: 4 hrs
Serving: 6-8

INGREDIENTS
- 3 pounds boneless pork shoulder
- 1 teaspoon garlic powder
- 1 teaspoon onion powder
- ½ teaspoon black pepper
- 1 teaspoon kosher salt
- ½ teaspoon ground allspice
- ½ teaspoon paprika
- ⅛ teaspoon ground cloves
- ½ teaspoon celery salt
- ½ cup water
- ½ teaspoon mustard powder

DIRECTIONS
1. Mix onion and garlic powder, salt, pepper, paprika, cloves and mustard powder in a small sized bowl.
2. Season the meat with the mixture. Transfer to crock pot
3. Add water to cover the meat.
4. Cover and cook on medium for 4 hours.
5. Shred with 2 forks. Serve hot. Side with coleslaw.

Nutrition Facts (Per Serving)
166 Calories
4.1g Total Fat
1.4g Saturated Fat
0g Trans Fat
83mg Cholesterol
260mg Sodium
490mg Potassium
0.7g Carbohydrates
0.2g Dietary Fiber
0.2g Sugars
29.8g Protein

35. Crock Pot Chinese Spare Ribs

Cook Time: 6 hrs
Serving: 4-6

INGREDIENTS
- 4 pounds pork spare ribs
- 1.5 Tablespoons ginger, grated
- 1 Tablespoon Chinese five spice
- ¼ cup dry white wine
- 4 garlic cloves, grated
- 2 Tablespoons tamari
- 1.5 Tablespoons apple cider vinegar
- 1.5 Tablespoon lemon juice
- 1 Tablespoon tomato paste
- 2 teaspoons honey

DIRECTIONS
1. Chop up the ribs into smaller sections. Place them in the slow cooker.
2. In a medium bowl, combine the ginger, Chinese 5 spice, white wine, garlic, tamari and vinegar. Mix well.
3. Pour the mixture over the ribs.
4. Cover and cook on low for 6 hours.

5. Serve warm. Side with rice or salad.

Nutrition Facts (Per Serving)
605 Calories
38.6g Total Fat
16.6g Saturated Fat
0g Trans Fat
151mg Cholesterol
1028mg Sodium
72mg Potassium
4g Carbohydrates
0.3g Dietary Fiber
2.5g Sugars
56g Protein

36. Paleo Easy Kalua Pork

Cook Time: 8 hrs
Serving: About 10

INGREDIENTS
- 5 pounds Pork Butt/Shoulder
- 3 teaspoon red Hawaiian Sea Salt
- 1 teaspoon liquid smoke

DIRECTIONS
1. Puncture the pork with a fork and place it in the slow cooker.
2. Add liquid smoke to the slow cooker and top it up with salt.
3. Cover and cook on low for 8 hours.
4. After cooking, once the meat is tender, shred and serve

Nutrition Facts (Per Serving)
366 Calories
12.7g Total Fat
4.2g Saturated Fat
0g Trans Fat
174mg Cholesterol
106mg Sodium

715mg Potassium
0.1g Carbohydrates
0g Dietary Fiber
0g Sugars
58.9g Protein

37. Paleo Easy Baby Back Ribs

Cook Time: 6-8hrs
Serving: 2-4

INGREDIENTS
- 3 pounds pork ribs
- ⅔ cup unsweetened apple sauce
- 2 cups tomato sauce
- 4 Tablespoons coconut aminos
- 4 Tablespoons apple cider vinegar
- 2 teaspoon hot sauce
- 2 Tablespoons Dijon mustard
- 1 Tablespoon ghee or organic butter
- ½ teaspoon black pepper
- 2 teaspoons chili powder
- 2 garlic cloves, minced
- ½ teaspoon cayenne
- 1 teaspoon paprika
- 1 medium yellow onion, diced
- Pinch of salt and fresh ground pepper, each

DIRECTIONS
1. In a saucepan, combine the vinegar, tomato sauce, mustard, pepper and hot sauce. Stir until combined.
2. Add the garlic, chilli powder, cayenne and paprika. Simmer for 15 minutes.
3. Cut ribs into smaller sections. Place in the slow cooker. Pour the sauce over the ribs. Coat evenly.

4. Cover and cook for 6-8 hours, until the meat is tender.
5. Serve hot.

Nutrition Facts (Per Serving)

474 Calories

36.2g Total Fat

14.7g Saturated Fat

0g Trans Fat

100mg Cholesterol

456mg Sodium

601mg Potassium

9.2g Carbohydrates

2.2g Dietary Fiber

5.4g Sugars

27.2g Protein

38. Slow Cooker Pork Tacos

Cook Time: 6 hrs
Serving: 8-10

INGREDIENTS

- 4 pounds pork shoulder/butt
- 2 Tablespoons chili powder
- 1 ½ teaspoon ground cumin
- 1 Tablespoon kosher salt
- ¼ teaspoon red pepper flakes
- ½ teaspoon ground oregano
- ½ cup beef broth
- A pinch of ground cloves
- 1 bay leaf

DIRECTIONS

1. Chop the pork into chunks.
2. In a bowl mix the salt, vinegar, chilli powder, cloves and red pepper flakes, mix well.

3. Season the meat with the mixture. Marinate anywhere from 2 hou hours.
4. Place the pork in the crock pot. Pour the broth over the meat. Ad bay leaf.
5. Cook on low for 6 hours, until meat is tender. Once cooked, remove the bay leaf.
6. Shred with forks. Serve with our favorite taco toppings.

Nutrition Facts (Per Serving)

334 Calories
11.7g Total Fat
3.8g Saturated Fat
0g Trans Fat
156mg Cholesterol
722mg Sodium
673mg Potassium
0.9g Carbohydrates
0.5g Dietary Fiber
0.1g Sugars
53.2g Protein

39. Paleo Slow Cooker Meatloaf

Cook Time: 4 hrs
Serving: 4-6

INGREDIENTS

- 2 pounds ground pork
- 2 cups diced onion
- 1 Tablespoon coconut oil or avocado oil
- ½ cup almond flour
- 2 eggs
- 1 Tablespoon garlic powder
- 2 Tablespoons maple syrup
- 2 teaspoons dried oregano
- 2 teaspoons fennel seeds

- 2 teaspoons ground sage
- 2 teaspoons red pepper flakes
- 1 teaspoon black pepper
- 2 teaspoons dried thyme
- 1 teaspoon sea salt
- 1 teaspoon paprika

DIRECTIONS

1. In a medium bowl, combine the seasoning; almond flour, garlic powder, oregano, fennel seeds, sage, red pepper flakes, thyme, sea salt, paprika. Mix well.
2. In a frying pan, heat the coconut oil and sauté the onions.
3. Place the ground pork in a bowl. Add the mixed seasoning. Crack in the egg. Mix all the ingredients together. Shape into a meat loaf form. Place in the crock pot.
4. Cover and cook on low for 3 hours. After 3 hours, remove the lid and pour maple syrup over the meat loaf. Re-cover and cook for another hour.
5. Slice and serve. Side with mashed potatoes, green beans.

Nutrition Facts (Per Serving)

235 Calories
7.7g Total Fat
3.3g Saturated Fat
0g Trans Fat
124mg Cholesterol
317mg Sodium
593mg Potassium
8.5g Carbohydrates
1.7g Dietary Fiber
4.7g Sugars
32.1g Protein

40. Paleo Pork Shanks

Cook Time: 4 hrs
Serving: 4-6

INGREDIENTS

- 3 pounds pork shanks, with bone
- 2 onions, diced
- 1 ½ Tablespoons avocado oil
- 4 garlic cloves, minced
- 2 cups carrots, diced
- 1 Tablespoon oregano leaves
- 3 cups mushrooms, chopped
- 2 Tablespoons basil leaves
- 2 teaspoon thyme leaves
- Juice squeezed from 2 limes
- 1 teaspoon sea salt
- 2 cups beef broth
- 2 cans diced tomatoes

DIRECTIONS

1. Sear the meat in a skillet until browned. Set aside.
2. Sauté the carrots, garlic, and onions in same skillet.
3. Add mixture to bottom of slow cooker. Place pork shanks on top.
4. Add thyme, salt, oregano, mushrooms, and lemon juice to slow cooker.
5. Cover and cook on medium for 4 hours.
6. Serve hot.

Nutrition Facts (Per Serving)

289 Calories
14.7g Total Fat
7.8g Saturated Fat
0g Trans Fat
78mg Cholesterol
642mg Sodium
430mg Potassium
15.2g Carbohydrates
3.5g Dietary Fiber
6.4g Sugars
27.5g Protein

LAMB

41. Paleo Lamb Stew

Cook Time: 4 hrs
Serving: 6-8

INGREDIENTS
- 2 pounds lamb steak
- 1 Tablespoon coconut oil
- ½ teaspoon salt
- 1 medium white onion, chopped
- 1 large carrot, sliced
- 1 teaspoon cinnamon powder
- 4 lemon peels, grated
- 1 ½ teaspoon coriander seed powder
- 1 ½ teaspoon cumin powder
- 1 teaspoon onion powder
- ½ teaspoon allspice
- 2 garlic cloves, sliced
- 2 Tablespoons lemon juice
- 1 Tablespoon tomato paste
- ¼ cup dried apricots, sliced
- 2 cups water
- 3-4 bay leaves
- ¼ cup almond slivers, toasted
- 1 teaspoon salt
- fresh parsley, chopped

DIRECTIONS
1. Warm up the crock pot, while in a large skillet, heat up the coconut oil. Sauté the onions for 2 minutes. Add the garlic, sauté for 1 minute. Add the lamb steak. Sear on all sides.

2. Transfer all the ingredients from the skillet to the warm crock pot. Add the lemon, carrots.
3. Cook on medium for 4 hours, or until the lamb is done.
4. Serve warm. Side with rice, or greens.

Nutrition Facts (Per Serving)
836 Calories
64.9g Total Fat
6g Saturated Fat
0g Trans Fat
41mg Cholesterol
279mg Sodium
247mg Potassium
28.1g Carbohydrates
13.6g Dietary Fiber
6.1g Sugars
41.7g Protein

42. Paleo Lamb Roast Root Veggies

Cook Time: 6 hrs
Serving: 8-10

INGREDIENTS
- 4 pounds boneless leg of lamb roast
- 1 Tablespoon ghee
- Pinch of sea salt, fresh ground pepper, each
- 6 garlic cloves, chopped
- ½ cup chicken broth
- 3 sprigs thyme
- 3 sprigs rosemary
- 2 large carrots, peeled, chopped
- ⅓ cup mustard, stone ground
- 2 Yukon gold potatoes, peeled, chopped
- 2 parsnips, peeled, chopped
- 1 small rutabaga, peeled, chopped

DIRECTIONS

1. In a small bowl, combine the garlic, thyme, rosemary and mustard. Stir well. Coat the lamb.
2. Place the lamb in the slow cooker. Add the vegetables. Pour the broth over the ingredients.
3. Cover and cook on low for 6 hours, or until the lamb is done.
4. Serve warm. Side with herb potatoes.

Nutrition Facts (Per Serving)

455 Calories
28.2g Total Fat
12.3g Saturated Fat
0g Trans Fat
3mg Cholesterol
191mg Sodium
387mg Potassium
16.3g Carbohydrates
3.5g Dietary Fiber
3.3g Sugars
35.2g Protein

43. Slow Cooker Lamb Curry Stew

Cook Time: 6 hrs
Serving:6-8

INGREDIENTS

- 2 pounds lamb stew meat
- 3 Tablespoons curry powder
- 2 teaspoons sea salt
- 2 teaspoons fresh ground pepper
- ½ Tablespoon paprika
- 1 cup chicken broth
- 4 stalks of celery, diced
- 3 medium sized carrots, chopped
- 4 garlic cloves, minced

- 1 medium yellow onions, diced
- 1 cup full fat coconut milk

DIRECTIONS

1. In a small bowl, combine the curry powder, sea salt, black pepper, paprika, and garlic cloves. Stir well.
2. Coat the lamb with the mixture.
3. Add carrots, celery, and onion to crock pot. Place lamb on top.
4. Pour the coconut milk and chicken broth over the ingredients.
5. Cover and cook on low for 6 hours, until lamb is tender.
6. Serve hot. Side with a salad.

Nutrition Facts (Per Serving)

349 Calories
19.8g Total Fat
12.5g Saturated Fat
0g Trans Fat
102mg Cholesterol
689mg Sodium
719mg Potassium
9.1g Carbohydrates
3.4g Dietary Fiber
3.3g Sugars
34.3g Protein

44. Paleo Crock Pot Leg of Lamb

Cook Time: 5 hrs
Serving: 6-8

INGREDIENTS

- 1 boneless leg of lamb
- Juice squeezed from 1 lemon
- 5 garlic cloves, chopped
- 1 Tablespoon rosemary, chopped
- 1 teaspoon coarse salt
- 1 teaspoon fresh ground pepper
- ½ cup chicken broth

- ½ cup wine
- ½ white onion, chopped
- 1 carrot, chopped
- 1 celery stalk, chopped

DIRECTIONS
1. In a small bowl, combine the lemon juice, garlic, rosemary, salt, pepper. Mix well. Coat the lamb with the mixture.
2. Add onion, carrot, and celery to crock pot. Place lamb on top.
3. Pour wine and broth over the ingredients.
4. Cover and cook on low for 6 hours, until lamb is tender.
5. Serve hot. Side with savory potatoes and a green vegetable.

Nutrition Facts (Per Serving)
234 Calories
9.7g Total Fat
2.7g Saturated Fat
0g Trans Fat
74mg Cholesterol
564mg Sodium
448mg Potassium
7.3g Carbohydrates
1.8g Dietary Fiber
2.1g Sugars
23.8g Protein

45. Crock Pot Lamb Shanks

Cook Time: 6 hrs
Serving: 2-4

INGREDIENTS
- 4 Lamb Shanks
- 2 large carrots, chopped
- 1 medium onion, chopped
- 2 celery stalks, chopped
- ¼ cup Arrowroot Flour

- 2 garlic cloves, minced
- 1 Tablespoon dried oregano
- 1 Tablespoon dried rosemary
- 1 Tablespoon dried thyme
- Pinch of sea salt and fresh ground pepper, each
- 2 Tablespoons tomato taste
- 15 ounce can diced tomatoes
- 2 cups beef stock

Garnish: chopped parsley

DIRECTIONS

1. Place the carrots, onion, and celery along the bottom of the crock pot. Sprinkle the arrowroot flour over the vegetables. Stir until they are coated.
2. Place the lamb shanks on top of the vegetables.
3. Season the lamb shanks with the garlic, oregano, rosemary, thyme, sea salt and fresh ground pepper.
4. Add the tomato paste, diced tomatoes. Pour in beef broth.
5. Cover and cook the lamb shanks for 6 hours.
6. Serve hot. Garnish with chopped parsley.

Nutrition Facts (Per Serving)

395 Calories
25.2g Total Fat
14.9g Saturated Fat
0g Trans Fat
72mg Cholesterol
575mg Sodium
1293mg Potassium
13.1g Carbohydrates
3.9g Dietary Fiber
5.6g Sugars
64.5g Protein

46. Graceful Paleo Lamb Stew

Cook Time: 6 hrs
Serving: 2-4

INGREDIENTS
- 1 pound lean lamb
- 1 teaspoon ground cinnamon
- 1 teaspoon ground coriander
- 1 teaspoon ground cumin
- Pinch of salt and fresh ground pepper
- 1 medium red onion, sliced
- 1 garlic clove, minced
- 2 cups tomatoes, diced
- 1 cup dried apricots

DIRECTIONS
1. Place the meat in a bowl and season with the cinnamon, coriander, cumin, salt and pepper.
2. Transfer lamb to crock pot. Add onion, garlic, tomatoes, apricot.
3. Cover and cook on low for 6 hours, until lamb is tender.
4. Serve hot. Side with rice or greens

Nutrition Facts (Per Serving)
242 Calories
8.1g Total Fat
2.5g Saturated Fat
0g Trans Fat
101mg Cholesterol
156mg Sodium
742mg Potassium
11g Carbohydrates
2.7g Dietary Fiber
7.7g Sugars
32.5g Protein

47. Paleo Lemon Artichoke Lamb

Cook Time: 6 hrs
Serving: 6-10

INGREDIENTS

- 8 pounds lamb chops
- 4 garlic cloves, chopped
- 1 large white onion, diced
- Zest of 2 lemons
- ¼ cup lime juice
- Pinch of salt and fresh ground pepper
- 2 Tablespoons ghee
- 4 lemons, sliced (2 for marinating, 2 for crock pot)
- 2 cups chicken stock
- 2 cans artichoke hearts
- 1 cup caper berries, rinsed
- 2 Tablespoons tapioca flour
Garnish: 2 Tablespoons chopped parsley

DIRECTIONS

1. In a glass dish, combine 8 cups of water, ¼ cup of salt and 2 sliced up lemons. Place the lamb chops in the mixture. Marinate in the fridge for 2-6 hours.
2. When ready to cook the lamb. Mix the garlic, onion, lemon zest, lime juice, salt and pepper in a bowl. Season the lamb.
3. In a large skillet, melt the ghee. Sear the lamb chops to create a crust on each side.
4. Place the lamb with the artichoke hearts, caper berries. Pour in the chicken stock.
5. Cover and cook on low for 6 hours.
6. Add sliced lemons and tapioca flour during last hour of cooking.
7. Serve hot. Side with salad, potatoes.

Nutrition Facts (Per Serving)

378 Calories
14.8g Total Fat
4.5g Saturated Fat
0g Trans Fat
165mg Cholesterol

428mg Sodium
531mg Potassium
4.6g Carbohydrates
1.5g Dietary Fiber
0.9g Sugars
53.8g Protein

48. Parsley Butter Roasted Lamb

Cook Time: 5 hrs
Serving: 10

INGREDIENTS
- 6 pounds of lamb meat
- ½ teaspoon kosher salt
- ½ teaspoon fresh ground pepper
- 1 cup water
- 1 whole lemon
- 2 Tablespoon chopped fresh parsley
- 4 Tablespoon butter/ghee

DIRECTIONS
1. Season the lamb with salt and pepper.
2. Place all the ingredients in your slow cooker.
3. Cover and cook on low for 5 hours.
4. Serve hot. Add butter, parsley, and lemon before serving.

Nutrition Facts (Per Serving)
365 Calories
16.4g Total Fat
6.7g Saturated Fat
0g Trans Fat
171mg Cholesterol
238mg Sodium
613mg Potassium
0.1g Total Carb
0.1g Dietary Fiber

0g Sugars
51g Protein

49. Slow Cooker Lamb Gizzard

Cook Time: 4 hrs
Serving: 4

INGREDIENTS
- 1 pound of lamb
- 3 garlic cloves, sliced
- bunch of cilantro, chopped
- ¼ cup Passata di Pomodoro
- 1 organic onion, diced
- ¼ cup water
- ½ cup white wine
- Pinch of sea salt

DIRECTIONS
1. Place all the ingredients in your slow cooker.
2. Cover and cook on low for 4 hours.
3. Serve hot. Side with rice or greens.

Nutrition Facts (Per Serving)
265 Calories
11.1g Total Fat
4.2g Saturated Fat
0g Trans Fat
98mg Cholesterol
102mg Sodium
418mg Potassium
3.6g Carbohydrates
0.7g Dietary Fiber
1.2g Sugars
30.4g Protein

50. Slow Cooker Lamb Cacciatore

Cook Time: 6 hrs
Serving: 4-6

INGREDIENTS
- 2 pounds of lamb
- ½ teaspoon black pepper
- 2 teaspoons kosher salt
- ¼ cup whole wheat flour
- 1-2 sprigs fresh rosemary
- 1 celery stalk, diced
- ¼ cup white wine
- ¼ cup cremini mushrooms, sliced
- 2 medium yellow onions, sliced
- 28 ounce can whole plum tomatoes

DIRECTIONS
1. Chop the lamb into chunks.
2. Place all the ingredients in your slow cooker.
3. Cover and cook on low for 6 hours.
4. Serve hot. Side with rice or greens

Nutrition Facts (Per Serving)
339 Calories
11.3g Total Fat
4g Saturated Fat
0g Trans Fat
136mg Cholesterol
919mg Sodium
770mg Potassium
10.4g Carbohydrates
1.7g Dietary Fiber
2.7g Sugars
44.6g Protein

Chicken

51. Paleo Slow Cooker Chicken Curry

Cook Time: 6 hrs
Serving: 2-4

INGREDIENTS
- 2 pounds of chicken breasts/thighs
- 2 cups full fat coconut milk
- 6 cups, your choice, fresh vegetables
- 1 Tablespoon cumin
- 1 cup tomato sauce
- 2 teaspoons ground ginger
- 2 teaspoons ground coriander
- 1 teaspoon cinnamon
- 2 teaspoons garlic powder
- 1 cup of water
- ½ teaspoon cayenne pepper
- Pinch of salt and fresh ground pepper, each

DIRECTIONS
1. Rinse the chicken, pat dry.
2. Dice the vegetables and chicken into chunks.
3. Place all the ingredients in your slow cooker.
4. Add the coconut milk, tomatoes, and spices.
5. Add the cup of water.
6. Cover and cook on low for 6 hours.
7. Serve hot. Side with rice or greens.

Nutrition Facts (Per Serving)
Calories 515
Total Fat 29.3g
Saturated Fat 15.2g
Trans Fat 0g
Cholesterol 119mg

Sodium 612mg
Potassium 460mg
Total Carb 23.2g
Dietary Fiber 3.1g
Sugars 14.1g
Protein 39.8g

52. Crock Pot Stuffed Chicken Breasts

Cook Time: 6 hrs
Serving: 2-4

INGREDIENTS
- 6 boneless chicken breasts
- ⅓ cup feta cheese, crumbled
- 1-2 teaspoons fresh oregano
- Pinch of salt, fresh ground pepper, each
- 1 Tablespoon olive oil
- ½ onion, diced
- 2 teaspoons minced garlic
- ¾ cup fresh spinach
- Juice of 1 lemon
- 2 pepperoncini peppers
- ½ red pepper, diced
- 1 cup chicken stock
- ½ cup white wine

DIRECTIONS
1. Rinse the chicken, pat dry.
2. Slice the chicken breasts ¾ open. Leave them attached.
3. In a large bowl, combine feta cheese, oregano, salt and pepper.
4. In a large skillet, heat the olive oil. Add the onion, cook 2 minutes. Add the garlic, cook 1 minute. Add the spinach. Heat until the spinach wilts.
5. Add the spinach mixture to bowl with feta cheese. Add the lemon juice, pepperoncini peppers, red pepper. Stir to combine.

2. Coat the chicken with oil. Season with salt and pepper.
3. Coat the potatoes with oil, salt and pepper. Wrap in foil.
4. Place the potatoes along bottom of crock pot.
5. Place chicken over the potatoes.
6. Cover and cook on low for 6 hours.
7. Serve hot. Side with greens.

Nutrition Facts (Per Serving)
443 Calories
15.3g Total Fat
4.1g Saturated Fat
0g Trans Fat
168mg Cholesterol
168mg Sodium
969mg Potassium
17.4g Carbohydrates
2.6g Dietary Fiber
0.3g Sugars
55.6g Protein

57. Paleo Salsa Chicken

Cook Time: 6 hrs
Serving: 6-8

INGREDIENTS
- 4 chicken thighs
- salad greens
- 1 pint of salsa
- shredded cheese (if you consume dairy)

DIRECTIONS
1. Rinse the chicken, pat dry.
2. Place the chicken, greens, and salsa in the crock pot.
3. Cook on low heat settings for 6 hours.
4. Garnish with cheese. Serve in a bed of lettuce.

Nutrition Facts (Per Serving)
310 Calories

175mg Cholesterol
146mg Sodium
497mg Potassium
2.1g Carbohydrates
0.6g Dietary Fiber
0.2g Sugars
66g Protein

59. Paleo Crock Pot Marinara Chicken

Cook Time: 4 hrs
Serving: 8-10

INGREDIENTS
- 4 pounds of chicken
- 1 jar marinara sauce
- 1 onion, diced
- 2 garlic cloves, diced
- ½ green pepper, diced
- 2 zucchini, diced
- ¼ cup basil
- Pinch of salt and fresh ground pepper, each
Garnish: Parmigiano Regiano, grated

DIRECTIONS
1. Rinse the chicken, pat dry.
2. Season the chicken with salt and pepper. Place in the crock pot.
3. Add the onions, garlic, green pepper, and zucchini.
4. Pour the marinara sauce over the ingredients.
5. Cover and cook on medium for 4 hours, until cooked through.
6. Shred the chicken with 2 forks.
7. Serve warm over favorite pasta. Top with Parmigiano Regiano.

Nutrition Facts (Per Serving)
319 Calories
6.1g Total Fat
1.6g Saturated Fat
0g Trans Fat

140mg Cholesterol
235mg Sodium
563mg Potassium
8.9gCarbohydrates
1.5g Dietary Fiber
5.4g Sugars
54.5g Protein

60. Paleo Chocolate Chicken

Cook Time: 6 hrs
Serving: 2-4

INGREDIENTS

- 2 pounds chicken breasts, bone in
- Pinch of sea salt, fresh ground pepper, each
- 2 Tablespoons ghee
- 1 medium onion, diced
- 4 garlic cloves, minced
- 7 medium tomatoes, peeled and chopped
- 2.5 ounces of dark chocolate, crumbled
- 5 dried chili peppers, finely chopped
- 1 teaspoon cumin powder
- ¼ cup Almond Butter
- ½ teaspoon cinnamon powder
- 1/2 teaspoon guajillo chilli powder
- Garnish: diced Avocado, chopped cilantro, and diced jalapeno pepper, seeds out

DIRECTIONS

Option: brown the chicken in a skillet prior to cooking in crock pot. (Melt the ghee, season the chicken with salt and pepper. Add to the skillet and sear on all sides until brown.)

1. Rinse the chicken, pat dry. (Do this before searing in skillet or placing in crock pot.)
2. Place all the other ingredients in the crock pot.

3. Cover and cook on low for 6 hours.
4. Serve warm. Garnish with avocado chunks, cilantro, and diced jalapeno.

Nutrition Facts (Per Serving)

477 Calories
20.6g Total Fat
10.7g Saturated Fat
0g Trans Fat
151mg Cholesterol
572mg Sodium
434mg Potassium
19.6g Carbohydrates
3.5g Dietary Fiber
14.1g Sugars
53.4g Protein

61. Paleo Coconut Curried Chicken

Cook Time: 5 hrs
Serving: 4-6

INGREDIENTS
- 3 pounds of chicken breasts/thighs
- 1 large onion, chopped
- 2 small carrots, chopped
- 2 garlic cloves, minced
- 1 Tablespoon curry powder
- 1 Tablespoon mustard condiment
- ½ cup coconut cream
- ½ cup chicken stock
- 2 Tablespoons ghee
- Pinch of salt
- 2 Yukon gold potatoes, peeled, chopped
Garnish: chopped parsley

DIRECTIONS
1. Rinse the chicken, pat dry.

2. Place all the ingredients, except the potatoes, in the crock pot. Stir well.
3. After 3 hours of cooking, add the potatoes.
4. Cover and cook on low for 4-5 hours, until chicken and potatoes are tender.
5. Serve warm.

Nutrition Facts (Per Serving)
377 Calories
25g Total Fat
11.4g Saturated Fat
0g Trans Fat
146mg Cholesterol
741mg Sodium
164mg Potassium
6.3g Carbohydrates
1.8g Dietary Fiber
2.7g Sugars
30.4g Protein

62. Crock Pot Buffalo Chicken

Cook Time: 6 hrs
Serving: 2-4

INGREDIENTS
- ½ pound chicken breast, boneless, skinless
- ½ pound chicken thighs, boneless, skinless
- ⅓ cup hot sauce
- 1 Tablespoon coconut aminos
- 2 Tablespoons ghee
- ¼ teaspoon cayenne
- ½ teaspoon garlic powder
- 4 small sweet potatoes, chopped
- ¼ - ½ cup of water
Garnish: ranch dressing, chives

DIRECTIONS
1. Rinse the chicken, pat dry.

3. Blend rest of ingredients in a food processor. Pour over chicken.
4. Cook on low for 4 hours.
5. Shred with 2 forks.
6. Serve hot. Side with baked potato.

Nutrition Facts (Per Serving)

217 Calories
6.3g Total Fat
1.6g Saturated Fat
0g Trans Fat
56mg Cholesterol
1041mg Sodium
970mg Potassium
19.6g Carbohydrates
4.5g Dietary Fiber
12.4g Sugars
22.1g Protein

65. Paleo Lemon Thyme Chicken

Cook Time: 4 hrs
Serving: 8-10

INGREDIENTS
- 4 pound chicken
- ¼ cup lemon juice
- 1 teaspoon dried thyme
- 2-3 bay leaves
- 5 garlic cloves, diced
- 1 teaspoon sea salt
- ¼ teaspoon black pepper
- ¼ cup of water

DIRECTIONS
1. Rinse the chicken, pat dry. Place in crock pot.
2. Pour lemon juice over the chicken. Season with thyme, salt and pepper. Add bay leaves, garlic. Add water to bottom of crock pot.
3. Cover and cook for 4 hours, until chicken is cooked through.

4. Serve hot. Side with salad.

Nutrition Facts (Per Serving)

276 Calories

5.6g Total Fat

1.6g Saturated Fat

0g Trans Fat

140mg Cholesterol

304mg Sodium

349mg Potassium

0.3g Carbohydrates

0.1g Dietary Fiber

0.1g Sugars

52.7g Protein

66. Paleo Slow Cooker Chicken Musakhan

Cook Time: 5 hrs

Serving: 6-8

INGREDIENTS

- 2.5 pounds chicken thighs, boneless, skinless
- 2 onions, sliced
- 1.5 teaspoons olive oil
- .5 ounce ground sumac
- 1 teaspoon cinnamon
- ¼ teaspoon ground allspice
- ¼ teaspoon ground cloves
- One pinch of saffron
- Handful of pine nuts
- Mint for garnish
- ¼ cup of water
- Pinch of salt and fresh ground pepper, each

DIRECTIONS

1. Rinse the chicken, pat dry.
2. In a small pot, combine the sumac, cloves, allspices, onion, olive oil, cinnamon and saffron and cook for 5 minutes.

3. Season the chicken with the cooked spices. Place in the crock pot. Add ¼ cup of water.
4. Cook on low heat settings for approximately 4-5 hours, until chicken cooked through.
5. Serve hot. Garnish with mint/pine nuts.

Nutrition Facts (Per Serving)

314 Calories
13.9g Total Fat
3.2g Saturated Fat
0g Trans Fat
126mg Cholesterol
124mg Sodium
413mg Potassium
3.5g Carbohydrates
0.9g Dietary Fiber
1.3g Sugars
41.8g Protein

Seafood

67. Paleo Crock Pot Chicken & Shrimp

Cook Time: 5 hrs
Serving: 8-10

INGREDIENTS
- 2 pounds chicken, boneless, skinless
- 1 pound peeled, deveined shrimp
- 1 large onion, chopped
- ¼ cup minced parsley
- 2 garlic cloves, minced
- 15 ounces tomato sauce
- ½ cup white wine
- 1 teaspoon dried leaf basil
- Pinch of salt and fresh ground pepper, each

Garnish: chives
Cook on stove: 1 pound fettuccine noodles to el dente

DIRECTIONS
1. Rinse the chicken, pat dry. Rinse the shrimp, pat dry.
2. Place in the crock pot.
3. Add the other ingredients to the crock pot.
4. Cover cook on low for 3hours, until chicken cooked.
5. Add the shrimp, cook 1 more hour.
6. Cook the fettuccine on the stove to el dente (slightly under cooked.) Add to the slow cooker last 30 minutes of cooking.
7. Serve in bowls. Garnish with chives.

Nutrition Facts (Per Serving)
371 Calories
7.5g Total Fat
1.6g Saturated Fat
0g Trans Fat
198mg Cholesterol

404mg Sodium
508mg Potassium
29.5g Carbohydrates
1g Dietary Fiber
2.4g Sugars
42.5g Protein

68. Paleo Salmon Head Soup

Cook Time: 3 hrs
Serving: 8-10

INGREDIENTS
- 1 salmon head, tail and any remaining pieces
- 1 minced bulb green garlic
- 1 small onion, diced
- 2 Tablespoons minced ginger
- 1 cup wakame
- ¼ cup tamari
- ¼ cup mirin
- 3 zucchinis, diced

Garnish: chives and chilies

DIRECTIONS
1. Place the salmon, along with ginger in slow cooker.
2. Cook on high for approximately 2 hours.
3. Add the meat with water in a stock pot.
4. Add ginger, tamari, mirin, onions, and garlic in to the stock pot.
5. Heat the soup for approximately 20 minutes, avoid boiling.
6. Add zucchini. Cook for 20 minutes.
7. Serve in bowls. Garnish with chives/chilies.

Nutrition Facts (Per Serving)
283 Calories
10.9g Total Fat
0g Saturated Fat
0g Trans Fat
143mg Cholesterol

670mg Sodium
243mg Potassium
7.1g Carbohydrates
1.4g Dietary Fiber
3.1g Sugars
37.6g Protein

69. Paleo Crock Pot Applesauce

Cook Time: 3 hrs
Serving: 2-4

INGREDIENTS
- 5 pounds of apples, a tart kind
- 1 whole vanilla bean
- ¼ cup honey
- ¼ teaspoon salt

DIRECTIONS
1. Rinse the apples. Peel and cut into chunks.
2. Place all the ingredients in the crock pot.
3. Cover and cook on low for 2-3 hours, until apples are cooked.
4. At the end of cooking, remove the vanilla bean. Stir the applesauce. (Eat warm or store in the fridge for up to 10 days.)

Nutrition Facts (Per Serving)
329 Calories
1.5g Total Fat
0g Saturated Fat
0g Trans Fat
0mg Cholesterol
236mg Sodium
309mg Potassium
81g Carbohydrates
7.8g Dietary Fiber
65.4g Sugars
2.8g Protein

70. Crock Pot Sweet Potato Poi Poi Uala

Cook Time: 2 hrs
Serving: 1-2

INGREDIENTS
- 3 sweet potatoes, halved
- ½ cup water
- 1 cup coconut milk
- ½ teaspoon sea salt

DIRECTIONS
1. Rinse the potatoes, and peel.
2. Cut into chunks. Place in crock pot.
3. Add water and salt.
4. Cover and cook for (approximately) 2 hours.
5. Once cooked, mash the potatoes further. Stir in coconut milk.
6. Serve immediately.

Nutrition Facts (Per Serving)
276 Calories
28.6g Total Fat
25.4g Saturated Fat
0g Trans Fat
0mg Cholesterol
488mg Sodium
318mg Potassium
6.8g Carbohydrates
2.7g Dietary Fiber
4g Sugars
2.8g Protein

71. Crockpot Split Pea Soup

Cook Time: 1 hr
Serving: 4-6

INGREDIENTS

- 1 ¼ cup split peas, dried
- 1 celery stalk, chopped finely (around same size of peas)
- ½ yellow onion, diced
- 2 garlic cloves, minced
- 2 carrots, chopped finely (around same size of peas)
- ½ teaspoon dried rosemary
- 2 teaspoons dried basil
- 1 teaspoon sea salt
- 1 bay leaf
- 4 cups of water
- ½ teaspoon black pepper

Garnish: chopped parsley

DIRECTIONS

1. Place all the ingredients in the crock pot.
2. Cook on low heat settings for 1 hour. Check doneness, cook longer if necessary.
3. Serve in bowls. Garnish with parsley.

Nutrition Facts (Per Serving)

326 Calories
1.2g Total Fat
0.2g Saturated Fat
0g Trans Fat
0mg Cholesterol
359mg Sodium
1026mg Potassium
58.6g Carbohydrates
24.2g Dietary Fiber
8.9g Sugars
22.7g Protein

72. Paleo Simple Slow Cooker Applesauce

Cook Time: 4 hrs
Serving: 2-4

INGREDIENTS
- 4 pounds of apples, peeled
- 2 pounds of pears, peeled
- 1 Tablespoon vanilla
- 4 cinnamon sticks

DIRECTIONS
1. Place all the ingredients in slow cooker.
2. Cover and cook on low for 4 hours, until apples and pears are tender.
3. Remove cinnamon sticks. Mash the mixture.
4. Serve immediately or refrigerate. (Up to 10 days.)

Nutrition Facts (Per Serving)
273 Calories
0.8g Total Fat
0g Saturated Fat
0g Trans Fat
0mg Cholesterol
6mg Sodium
536mg Potassium
71.2g Carbohydrates
16g Dietary Fiber
45.9g Sugars
1.7g Protein

73. Paleo Simple Vegetable Soup

Cook Time: 4 hrs
Serving: 2-4

INGREDIENTS
- 1 onion, diced

- 1 pound of carrots, peeled and chopped
- 1 head of celery, diced
- 1 pint of grape tomatoes, halved
- 6 red potatoes, cubed (You can leave peel on, just make sure to use a vegetable brush to clean them.)
- 4 cups of chicken broth
- 1 head kale, chopped (remove the spine)
- 2 teaspoons garlic powder
- Pinch of salt and fresh ground pepper, each

DIRECTIONS
1. Place all the ingredients in crock pot.
2. Cover and cook for 4 hours, until carrots, potatoes are tender.
3. Serve in bowls. Side with crusty rolls.

Nutrition Facts (Per Serving)
358 Calories
1.9g Total Fat
0.5g Saturated Fat
0g Trans Fat
0mg Cholesterol
858mg Sodium
2384mg Potassium
72.6g Carbohydrates
9.8g Dietary Fiber
14g Sugars
13.5g Protein

74. Easy Crock Pot Mexican Stew

Cook Time: 2 hrs
Serving: 2-4

INGREDIENTS
- 3 cups shredded carrots
- ½ head of cabbage, finely chopped
- 1 head of celery, finely chopped
- 1 large sweet onion, diced

- 2 zucchini, finely chopped
- 2 teaspoons tomato paste
- 28 ounce can diced tomatoes
- 3 teaspoons Polenta
- 5 garlic cloves, minced
- 1 cup cilantro, finely chopped
- 2 jalapenos, finely chopped
- 1 teaspoon chilli powder
- 4 cups of chicken broth
- Pinch of salt and fresh ground pepper, each
- 1 Tablespoon cumin
- 1 Tablespoon olive oil
- 2 cups of water

Garnish: avocado slices, cilantro

DIRECTIONS

1. In the crock pot, combine all the ingredients.
2. Cover and cook for 2 hours, until vegetables are tender.
3. Serve in bowls. Garnish with avocado and cilantro.

Nutrition Facts (Per Serving)

225 Calories
6.3g Total Fat
1.1g Saturated Fat
0g Trans Fat
0mg Cholesterol
837mg Sodium
1603mg Potassium
35.5g Carbohydrates
10.5g Dietary Fiber
17.9g Sugars
11.3g Protein

75. Paleo Crock Pot Summer Veggies

Cook Time: 2 hrs
Serving: 2-4

INGREDIENTS

- 2 cups Okra, sliced
- 1 ½ cups red onion, chopped
- 1 cup grape tomatoes, halved
- 2 ½ cups zucchini, sliced
- 2 cups yellow bell peppers, sliced
- ½ cup balsamic vinegar
- 1 cup mushrooms, sliced
- 2 Tablespoons basil, chopped
- ½ cup olive oil
- 1 Tablespoon thyme, chopped

DIRECTIONS

1. Place all the ingredients in the crock pot.
2. Cover and cook for 2 hours, until vegetables tender.
3. Serve in bowls, or as a side to a dish.

Nutrition Facts (Per Serving)

311 Calories
25.8g Total Fat
3.7g Saturated Fat
0g Trans Fat
0mg Cholesterol
19mg Sodium
642mg Potassium
19.4g Carbohydrates
4.8g Dietary Fiber
9.2g Sugars
3.9g Protein

Veg / Vegan

76. Slow Cooker Fig Apple Butter

Cook Time: 3 hrs
Serving: 8-10

INGREDIENTS
- 20 dried black figs, halved
- 1 cup apple cider
- 6 apples, peeled, and diced
- 3 Tablespoons cinnamon
- ½ cup honey
- ¼ teaspoon nutmeg
- ½ teaspoon ground cloves
- Pinch of sea salt

DIRECTIONS
1. Place all the ingredients in the crock pot.
2. Cover and cook for 3 hours.
3. Blend the mixture in a food processor. Serve or refrigerate.

Nutrition Facts (Per Serving)
461 Calories
1.7g Total Fat
0.2g Saturated Fat
0g Trans Fat
0mg Cholesterol
15mg Sodium
192mg Potassium
111.3g Carbohydrates
18.2g Dietary Fiber
30.6g Sugars
3.9g Protein

77. Paleo Easy Cabbage Apples

Cook Time: 4 hrs
Serving: 1-2

INGREDIENTS

- 2 tart apples, diced
- 1 large onion, sliced
- 1 medium cabbage, finely chopped
- ⅛ teaspoon ground pepper
- ½ teaspoon salt
- 1 cup apple juice
- ½ cup chicken stock
- 1 Tablespoon Butter or coconut oil
- 3 Tablespoons spicy mustard

DIRECTIONS

1. Place all the ingredients in the crock pot.
2. Cover and cook for 4 hours. Stir every hour.
3. Serve in bowls.

Nutrition Facts (Per Serving)

362 Calories
7g Total Fat
3.9g Saturated Fat
0g Trans Fat
15mg Cholesterol
1084mg Sodium
1223mg Potassium
76.5g Carbohydrates
18.2g Dietary Fiber
52.2g Sugars
7.4g Protein

78. Crock Pot Vegetable Korma

Cook Time: 4 hrs
Serving: 2-4

INGREDIENTS
- 1 large cauliflower, diced
- ½ cup frozen green peas
- 2 large carrots, diced
- ½ large onion, diced
- 1 cup green beans, diced
- ¾ can coconut milk
- 2 garlic cloves, minced
- 1 Tablespoon sea salt
- 2 Tablespoons curry powder
- 1 Tablespoon red pepper flakes
- 1 teaspoon garam masala
- 2 Tablespoons almond milk

DIRECTIONS
1. Place all the ingredients in the crock pot.
2. Cover and cook for 4 hours, until cauliflower is tender.
3. Sever in bowls.

Nutrition Facts (Per Serving)
251 Calories
17.7g Total Fat
12.9g Saturated Fat
0g Trans Fat
0mg Cholesterol
1736mg Sodium
505mg Potassium
22.2g Carbohydrates
7g Dietary Fiber
8.6g Sugars
6.2g Protein

79. Paleo Cauliflower Pumpkin Lentils

Cook Time: 6 hrs
Serving: 2-4

INGREDIENTS
- ½ head of cauliflower, chopped
- 1 large onion
- 1 Tablespoon coconut oil
- 1 Tablespoon ghee
- 3 garlic cloves, minced
- 1 Tablespoon grated ginger
- 2 teaspoons curry powder
- 2 cups peeled and diced pumpkin
- 1 teaspoon cumin powder
- 1 teaspoon turmeric powder
- 2 cups vegetable stock
- ½ teaspoon chilli flakes
- ½ cup lime juice
- ¾ cup coconut cream
- 2-3 Tablespoons sesame seeds
- Chopped coriander for garnish
- ½ Cauliflower, medium sized
- Sesame seeds/coconut cream for garnish

DIRECTIONS
1. Place all the ingredients in the crock pot.
2. Cover and cook for 6 hours.
3. Serve in bowls.

Nutrition Facts (Per Serving)
204 Calories
11.6g Total Fat
6.6g Saturated Fat
0g Trans Fat
13mg Cholesterol
349mg Sodium
656mg Potassium
26.4g Carbohydrates

9g Dietary Fiber
8.4g Sugars
5g Protein

80. Paleo Crock Pot Sarson Da Saag

Cook Time: 4 hrs
Serving: 1-2

INGREDIENTS
- 2 Tablespoons ghee
- 2 Tablespoons grated ginger
- 1 red onion, chopped
- 2 Serrano peppers, minced
- 2 Tablespoons minced garlic cloves
- 1 teaspoon coriander powder
- 2 teaspoons salt
- ½ teaspoon turmeric powder
- 1 teaspoon cumin powder
- ½ teaspoon black pepper
- ½ teaspoon Kashmiri chili powder
- 1 pound mustard leaves, chopped
- 1 pound of spinach

DIRECTIONS
1. In your crock pot, combine the ghee, garlic, Serrano peppers, onion and spices. Cover and cook on high for 1 hour.
2. In a large pot, add the mustard and spinach leaves. Stir continuously. Simmer for 4 minutes.
3. Blend the mixture in a food processor. Pour into the crock pot.
4. Cover and cook on low for 3 more hours.
5. Serve in bowls. Garnish with ghee.

Nutrition Facts (Per Serving)
380 Calories
23.5g Total Fat
8.8g Saturated Fat

0g Trans Fat
33mg Cholesterol
5073mg Sodium
1835mg Potassium
33.9g Carbohydrates
15.3g Dietary Fiber
5.8g Sugars
18.5g Protein

81. Paleo Jambalaya Vegan

Cook Time: 4 hrs
Serving: 2-4

INGREDIENTS
- 1 Tablespoon olive oil,
- 28 ounce can diced tomatoes
- 8 ounces seitan
- 8 ounces smoked vegan sausage
- ½ large onion, finely chopped
- ½ large green pepper, finely chopped
- 3 celery stalks, finely chopped
- 1 cup vegetable broth
- 2 garlic cloves, minced
- 1 Tablespoon miso paste
- 1 1/2 teaspoons Cajun seasoning
- ½ teaspoon dried thyme
- ½ teaspoon dried oregano
- 1 Tablespoon fresh parsley, chopped

DIRECTIONS
1. Place all the ingredients in the crock pot.
2. Cover and cook on low for 4 hours.
3. Serve in bowls, over rice.

Nutrition Facts (Per Serving)
387 Calories

7.2g Total Fat
1.7g Saturated Fat
0g Trans Fat
0mg Cholesterol
1602mg Sodium
1080mg Potassium
19.8g Carbohydrates
9.1g Dietary Fiber
7.6g Sugars
53.7g Protein

82. Paleo Easy Mashed Potatoes

Cook Time: 4 hrs
Serving: 4-6

INGREDIENTS
- 3 pounds red potatoes
- 4 Tablespoons butter
- 1 cup vegetable broth
- ½ cup coconut milk
- 3 garlic cloves, minced
- Pinch of salt and fresh ground pepper, each

DIRECTIONS
1. Rinse the potatoes. Cut the potatoes into bite-size pieces.
2. Place them in the slow cooker.
3. Add the remaining ingredients, except coconut milk.
4. Cover, cook on medium for 4 hours, until potatoes are tender.
5. Once cooked, mash the potatoes, add coconut milk.
6. Serve in bowls.

Nutrition Facts (Per Serving)
281 Calories
13g Total Fat
9.2g Saturated Fat
0g Trans Fat

20mg Cholesterol
199mg Sodium
1127mg Potassium
37.8g Carbohydrates
4.3g Dietary Fiber
3.1g Sugars
5.7g Protein

83. Paleo Easy Vegetable Casserole

Cook Time: 3 hrs
Serving: 10-12

INGREDIENTS
- 40 ounce can cannellini beans
- ¼ cup basil pesto
- 20 ounce can fava beans
- 4 garlic cloves, minced
- 1 medium onion, diced
- 16 ounces plain polenta, cut in slices
- 1 ½ teaspoons dried italian seasoning
- 8 ounces Italian cheese
- 1 large tomato, sliced
- 2 cups spinach
- 1 cup torn radicchio

DIRECTIONS
1. Combine all the ingredients in the slow cooker.
2. Cover and cook on low for 4 hours, until beans are tender.
3. Serve in bowls.

Nutrition Facts (Per Serving)
464 Calories
4.6g Total Fat
2.6g Saturated Fat
0g Trans Fat
11mg Cholesterol

233mg Sodium
1520mg Potassium
74.6g Carbohydrates
28.9g Dietary Fiber
4.8g Sugars
31.2g Protein

84. Paleo Vegetable Stew

Cook Time: 6 hrs
Serving: 10-12

INGREDIENTS
- 3 cups butternut squash
- 30 ounce can diced tomatoes
- 2 cups mushrooms, sliced
- 1 cup of water
- 15 ounces Great Northern beans
- 1 teaspoon dried italian seasoning
- 4 garlic cloves, minced
- ½ cup all-purpose flour
- ¼ teaspoon black pepper
- 2 Tablespoons parmesan cheese, grated
- ⅓ cup cornmeal
- 1 teaspoon baking powder
- 1 Tablespoon parsley
- 2 Tablespoons cooking oil
- 9 ounces italian green beans
- ¼ teaspoon salt
- Paprika

DIRECTIONS
1. Combine all the mentioned ingredients in the slow cooker.
2. Cover and cook on low for 6 hours.
3. Serve in bowls.

Nutrition Facts (Per Serving)
308 Calories
16.4g Total Fat
0.9g Saturated Fat
0g Trans Fat
1mg Cholesterol
57mg Sodium
709mg Potassium
29.8g Carbohydrates
8.4g Dietary Fiber
2.7g Sugars
14.2g Protein

85. Paleo Crock Pot Vegetable Curry

Cook Time: 6 hrs
Serving: 4-6

INGREDIENTS
- 4 carrots, sliced
- 1 cup of chickpeas
- 2 potatoes, cubed
- 1 onion, chopped
- ½ cup green beans
- 2 Tablespoons tapioca flour
- 3 garlic cloves, minced
- 1 teaspoon ground coriander
- 2 teaspoons curry powder
- ¼ teaspoon salt
- ½ teaspoon red pepper flakes
- 1 cup of vegetable broth
- ⅛ teaspoon ground cinnamon
- 1 small can of diced tomatoes

DIRECTIONS
1. Combine all the mentioned ingredients in a crock pot.

2. Cover and cook on low for 6 hours.
3. Serve in bowls.

Nutrition Facts (Per Serving)

381 Calories
5g Total Fat
0.6g Saturated Fat
0g Trans Fat
0mg Cholesterol
363mg Sodium
1351mg Potassium
69.2g Carbohydrates
17.7g Dietary Fiber
13.8g Sugars
18.2g Protein

86. Paleo Easy Mexican Minestrone

Cook Time: 6 hrs
Serving: 10-12

INGREDIENTS
- 1 cup of black beans
- 1 cup of vegetable broth
- 1 small can of stewed tomatoes
- 1 cup garbanzo beans, drained and rinsed
- 1 cup whole kernel corn, drained & rinsed
- 2 cups green beans
- 2 cups red potatoes, diced
- 1 cup salsa

Garnish: sour cream

DIRECTIONS
1. Combine all the ingredients in the crock pot.
2. Cover and cook on low for 6 hours.
3. Serve in bowls. Garnish with sour cream.

Nutrition Facts (Per Serving)

421 Calories

88. Paleo Juicy Cuban Pork

Cook Time: 6 hrs
Serving: 8-10

INGREDIENTS
- 3 ½ pound ham steak
- 1 teaspoon cumin seeds
- 1 Tablespoon minced oregano
- 4 garlic cloves, halved
- 1 ½ teaspoon sea salt
- ½ teaspoon ground oregano
- ¾ cup citrus juice
- 2 Tablespoons olive oil

DIRECTIONS
1. In a small bowl, crush and pound garlic and cumin seeds. Create a past with them. Mix in oregano, salt, and olive oil. Coat the ham steak with the mixture.
2. Place meat in Ziploc bag, refrigerate and marinate for 2-4 hours.
3. When ready to cook, place meat in crock pot. Add wet ingredients.
4. Cover and cook on low for 6 hours.
5. Serve warm. Side with salad.

Nutrition Facts (Per Serving)
591 Calories
31.7g Total Fat
10.5g Saturated Fat
0g Trans Fat
200mg Cholesterol
5099mg Sodium
1017mg Potassium
15g Carbohydrates
4.7g Dietary Fiber
1g Sugars
58.4g Protein

89. Crock Pot Balsamic Pork

Cook Time: 6 hrs
Serving: 6-8

INGREDIENTS

- 3 pound pork roast, boneless
- ½ teaspoon red pepper flakes
- 1 teaspoon garlic powder
- ⅔ cup balsamic vinegar
- ⅔ cup chicken broth
- 2 Tablespoons honey
- 2 Tablespoons Worcestershire sauce
- Dairy-Free Garlic Parsley
- Pinch of kosher salt

DIRECTIONS

1. Combine all the mentioned ingredients in the crock pot.
2. Cover and cook on low for 6 hours.
3. Serve warm. Side with mashed potatoes.

Nutrition Facts (Per Serving)

389 Calories
16.3g Total Fat
5.9g Saturated Fat
0g Trans Fat
146mg Cholesterol
224mg Sodium
754mg Potassium
7.3g Carbohydrates
0.1g Dietary Fiber
5.3g Sugars
49.2g Protein

90. Paleo Easy Vegetable Lasagna

Cook Time: 4 hrs
Serving: 6-8

INGREDIENTS
- 12-18 whole wheat oven-ready lasagne noodles
- 2-3 cups ricotta cheese
- 1 large can diced tomatoes
- 1 large can crushed tomatoes
- 3 large Portobello mushroom caps, sliced
- ¼ cup chopped baby spinach, chopped
- 1 small zucchini, sliced
- 3 garlic cloves, minced
- 1 teaspoon red pepper flakes
- 3-4 cups shredded mozzarella

DIRECTIONS
1. In a large bowl, combine the diced tomatoes, crushed tomatoes, mushrooms, zucchini, pepper flakes, garlic, and chopped spinach. Stir until well mixed.
2. Spoon a layer of sauce along bottom of crock pot.
3. Place a layer of noodles on top.
4. Spoon more sauce.
5. Spread a layer of ricotta cheese on top of the sauce.
6. Repeat until the sauce and ricotta are gone.
7. Top with mozzarella cheese.
8. Cover and cook on low for 4 hours.
9. Serve hot. Side with garlic bread.

Nutrition Facts (Per Serving)
322 Calories
7.4g Total Fat

4g Saturated Fat
0g Trans Fat
23mg Cholesterol
352mg Sodium
486mg Potassium
43g Carbohydrates
9.5g Dietary Fiber
9.2g Sugars
20.5g Protein

91. Paleo Crock Pot Sugar Ham

Cook Time: 2 hrs
Serving: 8-10

INGREDIENTS
- 8 pound ham, boneless
- ½ cup maple syrup
- 1 cup dark brown sugar
- 2 cups pineapple juice

DIRECTIONS
1. Combine all the ingredients in the slow cooker.
2. Cover and cook on low for 2 hours.
3. Slice and serve. Side with potatoes, greens.

Nutrition Facts (Per Serving)
476 Calories
20.9g Total Fat
7.1g Saturated Fat
0g Trans Fat
138mg Cholesterol
3159mg Sodium
772mg Potassium
ırbohydrates
tary Fiber
ırs
otein

92. Slow Cooker Pumpkin Red Lentils Chili

Cook Time: 5 hrs
Serving: 6-8

INGREDIENTS

- 30 ounce can kidney beans, drained
- 30 ounce diced tomatoes
- 2 cups vegetable broth
- 1 cup pumpkin puree (not pie filling)
- 1 cup dry split red lentils
- 1 small jalapeno pepper, diced (seeds in or out, your choice)
- 1 cup yellow onion, chopped
- 1 Tablespoon chili powder
- 1 Tablespoon cocoa powder
- ½ teaspoon cinnamon
- 2 teaspoons cumin
- 1 teaspoon kosher salt
- ⅛ teaspoon cloves

Garnish: cilantro, chopped

DIRECTIONS

1. Combine all the ingredients in the slow cooker.
2. Cover and cook on low for 5 hours.
3. Spoon into bowls. Side with pita bread, or tortilla chips.

Nutrition Facts (Per Serving)

302 Calories
2.2g Total Fat
0.5g Saturated Fat
0g Trans Fat
0mg Cholesterol
1033mg Sodium
1251mg Potassium
53.9g Carbohydrates
21.7g Dietary Fiber
9.6g Sugars
19.7g Protein

DESSERTS

93. Crock Pot Maple Glazed Pecans

Cook Time: 2 hrs
Serving: 6-8

INGREDIENTS
- 3 cups raw pecans
- ¼ cup maple syrup
- 2 teaspoons vanilla bean (scrape out the inside)
- 1 teaspoon sea salt
- 1 Tablespoon coconut oil

DIRECTIONS
1. Place all the ingredients in the crock pot.
2. Cover and cook on low for 2 hours. Stir occasionally.
3. Store in a jar after cooled down.
4. Note: if pecans are a bit sticky after cooking, cover a baking tray with parchment paper, slide them on the tray and pop them in the oven. Flip them over in 5 minute intervals.
5. Store in a sealed container, in the fridge for up to 9-10 months.

Nutrition Facts (Per Serving)
346 Calories
32.3g Total Fat
5g Saturated Fat
0g Trans Fat
0mg Cholesterol
313mg Sodium
201mg Potassium
14.8g Carbohydrates
4.5g Dietary Fiber
9.3g Sugars
4.5g Protein

94. Paleo Cinnamon Apple Quinoa

Cook Time: 2 hrs
Serving: 2-4

INGREDIENTS
- 1 cup rinsed quinoa
- 1 teaspoon vanilla extract
- 2 cups coconut almond milk
- ½ cup apple sauce, unsweetened
- 1 small apple, peeled and diced
- 2 teaspoons ground cinnamon
- 2-3 Tablespoons real maple syrup
- Pinch of salt

DIRECTIONS
1. Place all the ingredients in the crock pot.
2. Cook on low for 2 hours.
3. Serve warm with milk or slices of apple.

Nutrition Facts (Per Serving)
163 Calories
3.1g Total Fat
0.6g Saturated Fat
0g Trans Fat
0mg Cholesterol
65mg Sodium
298mg Potassium
30.3g Carbohydrates
4g Dietary Fiber
13.3g Sugars
3.5g Protein

95. Paleo Crockpot Pumpkin Butter

Cook Time: 4 hrs
Serving: 2-4

INGREDIENTS
- 4 cups pumpkin puree (not pie filling)
- 1 cup coconut sugar
- ½ cup ruby port
- 1 vanilla bean (inside scraped out)
- ¼ cup maple syrup
- 1 Tablespoon cinnamon
- Pinch of salt
- Pinch of cayenne pepper

DIRECTIONS
1. Add all the ingredients, except cinnamon, to the crock pot. Stir well until ingredients are combined.
2. Cook on low for 3 hours. Stir occasionally.
3. Remove the cover, add cinnamon. Cover and continue cooking for 1 hour.
4. Serve when warm or cooled down. Spread on toast.
5. Once cooled, it can be stored in a glass jar for up to 3 weeks in the refrigerator.

Nutrition Facts (Per Serving)
249 Calories
0.8g Total Fat
0.4g Saturated Fat
0g Trans Fat
1mg Cholesterol
54mg Sodium
523mg Potassium
57.9g Carbohydrates
7.1g Dietary Fiber
44.2g Sugars
2.5g Protein

96. Paleo Poached Pears

Cook Time: 4 hrs
Serving: 2-4

INGREDIENTS
- 6 pears, medium ripe
- ¼ cup maple syrup
- 2 cups orange juice
- 1 cinnamon stick, halved
- 5 cardamom pods
- 2 Tablespoons grated ginger

DIRECTIONS
1. Peel the pears. Core the pear.
2. Place the pears and rest of the ingredients in the crock pot.
3. Cook on low for 4 hours, until pears are fork tender.
4. Serve with whipped cream.

Nutrition Facts (Per Serving)
285 Calories
1.3g Total Fat
0.2g Saturated Fat
0g Trans Fat
0mg Cholesterol
8mg Sodium
697mg Potassium
71.4g Carbohydrates
10.7g Dietary Fiber
46.5g Sugars
2.8g Protein

97. Paleo Pumpkins Apples Raisins

Cook Time: 4 hrs
Serving: 2-4

INGREDIENTS
- 1 diced onion, large sized
- 2 gala apples, cubed
- ½ pumpkin, medium sized, cubed
- 2 garlic cloves, crushed
- 1 serrano pepper
- 2 Tablespoons garam masala
- ½ cup plump golden raisins
- 1 ½ cups chicken stock
- 1 ½ Tablespoon cumin seed
- ½ cup chopped cilantro
- ½ cup sliced almonds
- Pinch of salt
- 2 Tablespoons ghee
- 1 Tablespoon crushed chili peppers
- 12 curry leaves, diced

DIRECTIONS
1. In a skillet, melt the ghee. Sauté the onions and salt for 2 minutes, until they are translucent.
2. Add all the ingredients, including the onions, to the crock pot.
3. Cook on low for 4 hours, until pumpkin and apple fork tender.
4. Serve in bowls. Garnish with almonds/cilantro.

Nutrition Facts (Per Serving)
271 Calories
14.2g Total Fat
4.7g Saturated Fat
0g Trans Fat
16mg Cholesterol
1068mg Sodium
536mg Potassium

0g Trans Fat
55mg Cholesterol
837mg Sodium
519mg Potassium
23.4g Carbohydrates
4.7g Dietary Fiber
14.5g Sugars
6.3g Protein

99. Paleo Chunky Monkey Crock Pot Trail Mix

Cook Time: 2 hrs
Serving: 8-10

INGREDIENTS
- 2 ¼ cup raw walnuts, chopped
- 1 cup coconut flakes, unsweetened
- 1 cup cashews, raw, halved
- 2-3 Tablespoons coconut oil
- ⅓ cup coconut sugar
- 2 cups banana chips, unsweetened
- 1 teaspoon vanilla
- ¾ cup chocolate chips

DIRECTIONS
1. Coat the crock pot lightly with some of the coconut oil.
2. In the crock pot, combine vanilla, 2 tablespoons of the coconut oil, butter, sugar, coconut, and nuts.
3. Cover and cook on medium for 1 hour followed by low for 30 minutes. Stir occasionally.
4. Transfer mixture onto a parchment paper covered baking tray.
5. Sprinkle the chocolate chips and banana chips over the warm mixture. Let it cool down. Break into chunks.
6. Store in a zip lock bag in the fridge up to 10 days.

Nutrition Facts (Per Serving)
415 Calories
32.2g Total Fat
9.6g Saturated Fat
0g Trans Fat
3mg Cholesterol
15mg Sodium
408mg Potassium
26.9g Carbohydrates

4.3g Dietary Fiber
15.7g Sugars
10.4g Protein

100. Paleo Slow Cooker Carnitas

Cook Time: 6 hrs
Serving: 10-12

INGREDIENTS
- 5 pounds pork loin roast
- 1 teaspoon chili powder
- 1 teaspoon garlic powder
- 1 teaspoon kosher salt
- 1 teaspoon ground cumin
- Juice squeezed from 1 lemon
- Juice squeezed from 2 oranges
- 2 Tablespoons tomato paste
- 2 cups chicken stock
- 4 garlic cloves, crushed
- 1 Tablespoon Adobo seasoning
- Paleo-friendly oil of choice

DIRECTIONS
1. In a large skillet, heat up 1 tablespoon of coconut oil. Sear the roast on all sides until a nice crust appears.
2. Place the roast in the crock pot. Add the remaining ingredients.
3. Cover and cook on low for 5 hours, check doneness. Continue cooking if necessary. Check at 30 minute intervals.
4. Shred the meat with 2 forks.
5. Serve hot. Side with potatoes, green vegetable.

Nutrition Facts (Per Serving)
333 Calories
14.7g Total Fat
5.3g Saturated Fat
0g Trans Fat

122mg Cholesterol
372mg Sodium
724mg Potassium
4g Carbohydrates
0.9g Dietary Fiber
2.8g Sugars
43.8g Protein

101. Paleo Jerk Styled Chicken

Cook Time: 5 hrs
Serving: 6-8

INGREDIENTS
- 4 pounds of chicken, with bone, skin-on
- 2 habanero chilies, diced
- 6 green onions, finely chopped
- ½ cup pineapple juice
- 1 Tablespoon sliced ginger
- 1 Tablespoon minced thyme
- 5 garlic cloves, minced
- ¼ teaspoon cardamom
- 2 teaspoons allspice
- 2 limes, sliced
- 1 cinnamon stick
- Pinch of salt and fresh ground pepper, each

DIRECTIONS
1. In a food processor, combine the habanero, onion, garlic, ginger, cardamom, pineapple juice, allspices, thyme, salt and pepper. Pulse until the ingredients are combined.
2. Spread the seasoning over the chicken. Place in the crock pot.
3. Cover and cook on low for 5 hours.

4. If you want an extra crispiness, after finished cooking in the crock pot, place on a baking tray and broil the meat for 10 minutes per side.
5. Serve hot. Side with rice, lemon slices, fresh green onions.

Nutrition Facts (Per Serving)
368 Calories
7.2g Total Fat
2g Saturated Fat
0g Trans Fat
175mg Cholesterol
149mg Sodium
521mg Potassium
6.1g Carbohydrates
1.3g Dietary Fiber
2.3g Sugars
66.4g Protein

Conclusion

Well you made it to the end. I hope this book helped in your quest to live a healthy lifestyle by incorporating Paleo diet. Hopefully, it helps achieve weight loss, as well as motivate you to stay with the Paleo lifestyle.

Paleo meals cooked in crock pots/slow cookers won't just save you precious time but also the hassle of being physically present in the kitchen. You arrive home from work to delicious and healthy meals. You can even prepare the ingredients the night before.

Each recipe listed in the book will provide nutrients your body needs to function. Your body won't be deprived of any micronutrient or macronutrient. It will also assist in achieving a balance between saturated and unsaturated fats that we consume through the day. Paleo isn't a temporary weight loss program, but a lifestyle for long term that provides sustained results.

CPSIA information can be obtained
at www.ICGtesting.com
Printed in the USA
LVOW09s0413020118
561465LV00004B/157/P